Personalizing Learning in the 21st Century

Personalizing Learning in the 21ˢᵗ Century

Edited by

Sara de Freitas and Chris Yapp

Published by Network Educational Press
PO Box 635
Stafford
ST16 1BF
www.networkpress.co.uk

First published 2005
© Sara de Freitas and Chris Yapp 2005

ISBN-13: 978 1 85539 202 1
ISBN-10: 1 85539 202 X

Black, P. and Wiliam, D. (1998), 'Assessment and Classroom Learning', *Assessment in
Education*, 5(1), pp. 7–74. Reprinted by permission of Taylor & Francis Ltd.
The website for this journal is at www.tandf.co.uk/journals.

Strong, R.W., Thomas, E., Perini, M.J. and Silver, H.F. (Feb. 2004), 'Creating a Differentiated
Mathematics Classroom', *Educational Leadership* 61(5), p. 74. © ASCD, Alexandria, VA.
Reprinted by permission. The Association for Supervision and Curriculum Development is a
worldwide community of educators advocating sound policies and sharing best practices to
achieve the success of each learner. To learn more, visit ASCD at www.ascd.org.

Managing editor: Helen Bannister, Pencil-Sharp Editors
Design, typesetting and cover: FiSH Books Ltd

Printed in Great Britain by MPG Books Ltd, Bodmin, Cornwall

CONTENTS

FOREWORD

Personalization

At first the word and concept are unattractive. Personalization for many brings to mind cufflinks, t-shirts and car number plates – a kind of insecure pretentiousness that offends good taste.

Yet 'personalization' bears another meaning – the preference for the 'personal' rather than the 'impersonal'.

In that sense, and in an age where the impersonality of Orwell's 'Nineteen Eighty-Four' appears to loom ever closer, the present government's attempts to emphasize the importance of 'personalization' in the provision of public services, especially education and schooling, is welcome. After all, there is a great danger in the provision of health, education and the police through very large organizations, that provision which is universal inevitably becomes the same thing for everybody and 'one size fits all' rather than something tailored to the needs of individual differences. In short, universal services have to be 'personalized' rather than uniform.

In schools there is a myriad of practices which can be either personal or impersonal. The teacher in the classroom, for example, either does or does not know the pupils. If she seeks to be successful with every youngster, she must know them well. The wise teacher spends a lot of preparation time putting names to faces and using those names. She determines the seating plan – rather than allowing free choice – to assist in the process and the behaviour of the class generally. She remembers birthdays; she uses children's past successes ('—Class 6 ... didn't Jane help us with this problem last week? Sam can you show us how ...') to enlist collective interest in the solving of a particular learning challenge. And of course she shares questions fairly and in a way that affirms confidence. If she's a primary teacher, she organizes the classroom so that every child has an allotted task. Her marking practices ensure, for example in secondary school, that at least once a term every member of the class gets extensive private feedback on one piece of work, even if time dictates that on other occasions she is necessarily more truncated in her marking. She practises what's now called 'assessment for learning' so that each and every child in her class knows what the next stage of their learning is and what they need to do to complete it successfully. She tries to emphasize the pupil's 'own previous best' as a measurement rather than the normative. She notices and acknowledges by name children about the school – in the corridors at lunchtime and in the playground. She frequently pauses for conversation. If she has a youngster with whom she's finding it difficult to make a meaningful relationship, she'll find his private interest and collect something over the weekend and stop to show or give him the item on a Monday morning and say 'Sean, I saw this and thought of you.' All this and much more – how to use tutorial time to good effect, for example – are the stock in trade for successful teachers committed to personalization.

The context of the school in which the teacher works affects the likelihood of her behaving in a personal rather than an impersonal way. She'll know and be known well by her headteacher. Her efforts will be frequently acknowledged publicly and privately by middle and senior managers. She'll see headteachers and their colleagues modelling the 'personalized' behaviour which she herself is attempting: handwritten letters of thanks, birthdays remembered, acts of unexpected kindness, the receipt of thanks after the successful completion of a task and the taking away of blame when she takes a risk that has not come off. If she's in a large secondary school, she'll be contributing actively to the 'House' or 'Year' register of youngsters 'at risk' of not taking advantage of her education and – even more importantly – taking part in activities that grow such pupils' 'resilience'. She'll be taking part in and be a contributor to one or more of the extra-curricular opportunities that the school offers. In all likelihood she'll go on a 'residential' with one of the many groups of youngsters, all of whom know of and are encouraged to take up their 'entitlement' to such experiences, which increase the likelihood of schooling being personal and worthwhile.

The leaders of the school also arrange things to emphasize and live out the example of being personal. One head of a large (1,300 boys) secondary school teaches every Year 7 class once a week and in his lessons teaches what he calls the legacy of the school – that the pupils inherit the legacy and how they will, in their turn, contribute to that legacy. It's a part of the citizenship programme; he shares the task with his deputy. The high points of the year include a residential for all Year 7 pupils, along with tutors, year head, head and deputy, and a cultural presentation. By the end of the year, the head and the deputy, know all Year 7 pupils by name – and hence, over time, the whole school. Meanwhile the head of a primary school writes three letters a week to Key Stage 1 pupils inviting them to tea. By the end of the year she too knows every child and keeps up the process of emphasizing the uniqueness of each pupil.

Organizationally the timetable and a curriculum in a secondary school can assist or not in the process of personalization. A school that imposes the need for a teacher to get to know 350 pupils because she has to teach that number of pupils in different groups rather than, say, 150 isn't helping. Nor is a timetable that imposes the same curriculum on everyone, as opposed to allowing some choice – albeit guided. Grouping practices also affect personalization, as do the subliminal messages conveyed by who is celebrated at awards evenings and for what. Meantime the primary headteacher is mindful of the teacher working with the learning assistant so that each plays a role and shares the task of really knowing and having a worthwhile relationship with every child. For as one Victorian once commented, 'Unless a child has at least one worthwhile relationship with a member of staff they are not really at school. They may be physically present but they are not there.'

In the last few years, the advent of Information and Communication Technology (ICT) has opened up a whole new world full of possible successes and pitfalls for 'personalization'.

Clearly in the world of severe disability, the technologies have overcome large learning barriers of the senses – including movement – and of communication. But the possibilities of e-tutoring and e-learning in the community are now emerging, as is the easing of time-consuming tasks within the school as e-learning platforms integrated with management information systems enable teacher and learner alike to access essential information and learning situations.

In short, 'personalization' can be a kind of litmus test for all schools to use to make sure that they are making all of their community feel special and, in the process, more confident that their potential is enormous. Personalization is no mere theory: personalization is as personalization does.

Tim Brighouse
Chief Advisor for London Schools

Introduction to the Contributions – Personalization: Is there a consensus?

Over the last two to three years the term personalization in learning has been the subject of many speeches, conferences and working groups. On 4 July 2005, 30 people were invited to meet at the Design Council in London under the auspices of the London Knowledge Lab, the Lab Group and the Association for Learning Technology (ALT) to discuss the state of play regarding personalized learning. Drawn from policy, practice, industry and academe it was not expected that any 'silver bullet' would emerge. It was felt that these groups had been meeting in their own circles to discuss the issues around personalized learning rather than meeting all the stakeholders in the debate. Each was asked to prepare a position paper for the event. After an opening presentation by Diana Laurillard, Head of the E-learning Strategy Unit at the Department for Education and Skills (DfES), there was an open discussion on the theme 'Personalization: is there a shared vision?' The aim was to identify the areas that needed to be debated, researched and understood to achieve an actionable consensus on the issue of personalization. The notes below reflect the areas that arose in this discussion.

Before we get to a view on a shared vision for personalized learning, it is important to discuss whether we are agreed on what it takes to be, and what it means to be, a good learner. In this area there was felt to be a strong consensus about the learner as an active agent rather than a passive recipient of learning. From here the question arises about whether we mean personalization *by* the learner or personalization *for* the learner. The balance between *for* and *by* probably does change with age and stage, but how? This, in turn, leads us to reflect on how the learner's voice is considered in the process of personalization. It was agreed that the comfort with which the rising generation adopts new technologies was not fully understood or appreciated by adults in general as well as teachers, but that there was a danger of putting the ICT cart before the learning horse. It is quite clear that this puts a heavy premium on the adaptability of teachers and teaching practice.

All of this begs the question 'why personalize in the first place?' It is quite easy to claim that this is either political froth or political leadership but the political processes of wishing to create evidence-based policy to inform a process of transforming learning are non-trivial. For those engaged in the 'supply-side' of delivering education, it is difficult to discern a vision or where it might emerge from for ubiquitous technologies to underpin a system-wide transformation of the experience of education. Creating a leadership cohort within education policy and institutions to engage in building the will and capacity to lead the process of transformation is, however, far more important and challenging if any of the aspirations are to be realized.

Part of this challenge is the articulation not just of the vision of personalization of learning, but also the value system that underpins it, that is to say the moral purpose of personalizing learning. If the aim is to create a system of learning that personalizes 'for the many not for the few', and that makes the systems of learning flexible enough to realize the potential of all learners, then this needs to be made explicit. If the aim is to excite and motivate teachers and leaders across all institutions to challenge and reflect on their new needs as learners themselves, then this needs to be made explicit. If this is not the aim, then what is it? The question arises as to whether the support of learners requires greater teamwork among teachers and the extent to which this is recognized in recruitment, training and retention strategies for the next generation of teachers.

Personalizing learning and leading the transformation is a long-term journey. To sustain energy and momentum and to build successes and evidence to support the ongoing programme will require much greater feedback between all the 'stakeholders'. Technology provides the capability to make this feedback easier, quicker and above all scalable, but the changes in working practice required to benefit from investments in such technologies are less well understood. The observation was made that children familiar with these technologies seem to have a different balance between formal and informal learning than adults raised prior to the emergence of these technologies. This balance is reflected in their willingness to ask questions, share experience and engage. As earlier observed, these are all characteristics of the learner as an active participant which is central to our understanding of the 'good learner'. Can or should we capture this informal learning within our new notions or does this risk instrumentalizing informal learning?

The truth, however, is that in all life, not just in education and learning, we as individuals and in communities have to operate inside constraints, boundaries and limits on our freedom of action. Time and money are two obvious such constraints. Given the long-term nature of the challenges, this will require many compromises and acknowledgment of responsibility at every level of policy and practice as well as every age and stage of the learner.

An important feature of the personalization of learning is the accessibility of learning, as much as the accessibility of learning roles. The use of ICTs to overcome barriers posed by a variety of disabilities provides opportunities to extend learning to groups that have been difficult to reach with traditional methods.

To those practising teachers today, the most important such constraints are curriculum and assessment. Personalized learning provides many challenges to curriculum, challenging subjects and subject boundaries, but assessment may well be the greater hurdle. There is a growing belief in the importance of formative assessment, and a belief that this, more than changes in summative assessment, will be the key to unlocking the potential that personalization aspires to realize. Here again systems of feedback between teacher and learner need to be richer than we have yet fully explored. One area of growing interest is that of e-portfolios. It can be argued that these potentially increase learner voice and responsibility in managing their own learning needs.

Personalized learning holds the danger of creating an image of the learner as an isolated individual. The firm consensus was that learning is a social process. We can see this frequently with young people's use of 'social technologies' such as blogging or SMS texts. With adults, the use of ICTs to support and develop 'communities of practice' provides a potential route forward.

The enthusiasm, passion and commitment for this topic among the participants was quite clear. A recognition of the difficulties and unknowns was clearly discernible in the discussions. At this stage there are more questions than answers, that is quite clear, but the areas which genuinely need to be researched and those which are more a matter of policy and implementation were perhaps more widely agreed than might have been expected.

The papers of these participants which make up the bulk of this book, we believe, can help all of us, whichever role we play in learning, to reflect and understand the views and state of thought across all the stakeholders affected by these ambitions. We are all learners, with personal needs, and will need to participate fully in the transformation of learning.

Sara de Freitas and Chris Yapp
Birkbeck College, University of London, 2005

List of Abbreviations

Becta	British Educational Communications and Technology Agency
CPD	continuing professional development
DfES	Department for Education and Skills
EAZ	Education Action Zone
FE	Further Education
HE	Higher Education
HEFCE	Higher Education Funding Council for England
HEI	Higher Education Institution
ICDC	International Certificate in Digital Creativity
ICT	Information and Communication Technology
ILT	Information and Learning Technology
IT	Information Technology
JISC	Joint Information Systems Committee
MIS	Managment Information Systems
MLE	Managed Learning Environment
NIACE	National Institute of Adult Continuing Education
NVQ	National Vocational Qualification
LEA	Local Education Authority
PDA	Personal Digital Assistant
SMS	Short Messaging Service
THES	Times Higher Education Supplement
VAK	visual, auditory and kinesthetic
VLE	Virtual Learning Environment

THE CHALLENGE: ICT AND PERSONALIZED LEARNING

1

Harnessing Technology to Personalize the Learning Experience

Diana Laurillard

> f we manage the process of embedding properly, we should be able to infuse the whole education process with the added value that technology brings, thus enhancing the quality of provision at all levels.

Personalizing learning in the twenty-first century

Our aims for a twenty-first-century education system were outlined in the Government's five-year strategy for education and children's services (DfES, 2004). The five principles for reform highlighted personalization and choice; flexibility and independence in the provision of learning; a service opened up to a wider range of providers and forms of cross-organizational collaboration; a major focus on staff development; and an approach that fosters more partnerships.

The strategy for reform is carried through each age and stage of education and children's services, from the children's strategy through the schools, 14–19, higher education, to skills and lifelong learning strategies.

The Department's e-strategy plays a crucial part in supporting these strategies. We have identified four challenging objectives against which the success of the e-strategy should be judged:

- to transform the process of teaching, learning and individual support
- to engage the hard-to-reach groups
- to open up greater possibilities of cross-organizational collaboration
- to improve efficiency and effectiveness.

These will be difficult to achieve, but we do know that ICT can be used successfully and effectively, in many different ways, to benefit all the participants in the learning, teaching and development communities. So why not push for the challenging objectives?

We have great ambitions for an improved education system. The scope and scale of what yet needs to be done is enormous, especially if we look beyond the UK to the wider world. There are 40 million children in sub-Saharan Africa who have no primary schooling, for example – how could we ever hope to train the teachers they need without recourse to a technology that can achieve quality of provision on a large scale? Across the world there are millions more with no access to higher education who could also be served through the wise application of technology. And at home there are still many people with talent who are failed by our education system, in both senses of that word – hence the focus on a more personalized system. So our strategy must direct ICT toward helping to secure our most ambitious ideals.

3

ICT is expensive and complex, so the objectives for its use are stated in the most challenging possible way – if it does not have truly transformational effects on the quality and practice of education, then we should not be using it.

Harnessing technology

The UK e-strategy (DfES, 2005) outlines the sector-specific actions that are needed if we are to achieve the potential of ICT, and these are specified for schools, post-16, higher education, and children's services. However, we will only really harness technology to our aims if we act collectively. Therefore, the strategy begins by specifying the priorities at system level:

- to support all citizens with integrated information about education and children's services

- to support children and learners of all ages with online personalized advice and guidance

- to bring together education and industry to create more personalized learning activities.

To make this possible, we must also specify the priorities for practitioners and leaders:

- to provide good quality training, with assured ICT access, and online communities of practice

- to provide models for ICT maturity to help leaders plan the progress of their organization.

Finally, we must prioritize the technology that makes possible this greater integration and collaboration. We need:

- to provide a common digital infrastructure that achieves efficient ICT usage for all.

In this way, we hope to use ICT and e-learning to transform the quality of education and children's services through a cross-sector collaborative approach to making the best use of the technology.

If we manage the process of embedding properly, we should be able to infuse the whole education process with the added value that technology brings, thus enhancing the quality of provision at all levels.

Using ICT and e-learning to support personalization

Personalization can mean many different things for a learner, according to their stage on the learning journey through the education system, and ICT and e-learning contribute to personalization throughout. Figure 1.1 illustrates a way of representing the very wide range of its applications within education.

Prior to their engagement with the education system, learners will ask 'why should I learn?' Whether the learner is at pre-school stage and we are persuading a parent, or they are a lifelong

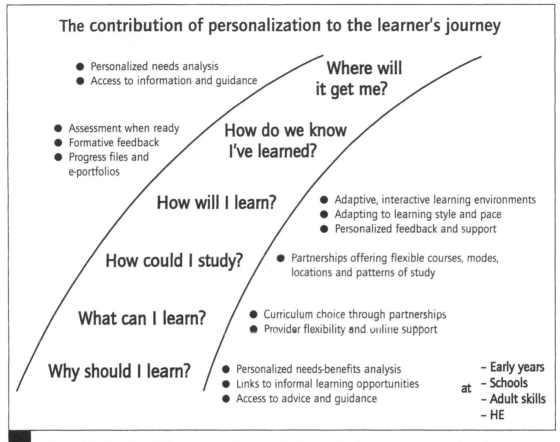

Figure 1.1: Showing different types of personalization as the learner encounters the education system; applicable at any age or stage of education.

learner late in their professional career, e-learning can make the entry easier, through, for example: more accessible information and guidance; online links from their informal interests to informal learning and later to formal learning opportunities; and a personalized interactive checklist to help decide why education might be useful to them.

The next decision is what to learn, and wider curriculum provision is possible from one institution if it uses ICT to create partnerships with other providers, thus extending its curriculum through online tutors and resources. In this way a school, college or university can tailor its curriculum to meet a much wider range of learners' needs.

The mode of study can be much more flexible with e-learning and can be designed to fit the learner's circumstances, mixing online and campus-based, part-time and full-time, continuous and interrupted study, exploiting online collaborative networks across institutions, the workplace and the home to achieve this.

The experience of learning should be more interactive, adaptive, collaborative, creative – and fun. e-Learning blended with traditional methods offers a much richer and more varied learning experience because it contributes a greater degree of active learning. And it can be personalized in the sense that a well-designed e-learning resource can diagnose and adapt to the learner's needs much more than is possible without ICT.

Knowing what they have achieved is very important to learners, not just because grades are a ticket to the next stage. They need assistance, guidance, hints and feedback as they are learning, and they need the right judgement of their achievements to know what they should focus on. A greater variety of assessment methods and more formative feedback, along with the traditional forms of assessment, will provide a much better service to learners.

Finally, once the achievement is accredited, the learner will need to know what they can do with it, or what more they need for their desired next step. Again, online information and advice adapted to their current position will help them make the right decision.

All these points can be interpreted for each age group of learners – early years, school, Higher Education (HE) and lifelong learning. They illustrate the complexity of the concept of personalization. In general, it means optimizing the learning experience for every learner. This would be prohibitively labour intensive if we seriously tried to achieve it with teachers alone. But ICT and e-learning make personalization feasible, in all these different ways.

Where is research needed?	Basic research & development	Action research	Planning and management
Personalised neeeds analysis Access to information and guidance		✓	✓
Assessment when ready Formative feedback Progress files and e-portfolios	✓	✓	✓
Adaptive, interactive learning environments Adapting learning needs Personalized feedback and support	✓ ✓ ✓		
Partnerships offering flexible courses, modes, locations and patterns of study	✓	✓	✓
Curriclum choice through partnerships Provider flexibility and online support			✓ ✓
Personalized needs-benefits analysis Links to informal learning opportunities Access to advice and guidance	✓		✓ ✓

Figure 1.2: Showing the forms of personalization most likely to need basic research and development, those more likely to need action research by practitioners, and those needing simply good professional management

Where is research needed?

Some aspects of personalized learning need basic research studies to be carried out, building on current theories and research findings. Some need action research and some need simply good planning and management.

Action research means practical improvement through trialling and testing innovative ways of providing the best services to students and learners. This is an aspect of good professionalism, and could be part of what every teacher, lecturer and support staff member would expect to do, if given the mandate to do it.

Other aspects of personalization need careful planning and management of resources. They will be improved through practice, of course, but the main task is to take the decision to do it and plan it properly from the outset.

Figure 1.2 suggests which forms of personalization need basic research, which need action research by the practitioners and which simply need good planning.

The point of this is to spread the innovation effort among all the professionals involved in e-learning and education: focus the research effort where it is most needed on understanding learner needs; distribute the responsibility for improving practice among all practitioners; and locate with leaders and managers the responsibility for the resourcing and system changes needed.

Using pedagogy to support personalized learning

Turning to those aspects of personalization that need basic research and development, it is clear that we will need a new understanding of the pedagogies appropriate for a twenty-first-century education system if we are to make real progress with personalized learning. Traditional methods have not achieved enough. The wider availability of new technology means that we have the opportunity – and the responsibility – to explore new approaches to teaching and learning. The familiar and effective teaching methods of listening, reading, writing and class discussion will, of course, remain important, but our teaching institutions ought to be advancing beyond the traditional formats that are still so prevalent.

Over the last hundred years or so, learning theorists such as Dewey, Piaget, Vygotsky, Bruner, Freire, Pask, Winograd, Papert, Resnick, Seely Brown, Marton, Biggs, and Lave have expressed the nature of active learning in a variety of ways, from constructivism, to discovery learning, to meta-cognition, to situated learning … but they all have in common the focus on the learner as being an active participant in the process.

The key educational theorists who have contributed to an understanding of the learning process, rather than simply offering an exhortation to teachers (e.g. Skinner, Gagne), generally share this opinion: that learning must be active on the part of the learner. Knowledge is a social construct, more an emergent property of the interaction between people than an abstract entity to be transmitted from one to another.

So learning is a social process in which learners must take part by:

- being engaged in goal-oriented tasks
- practising skills
- exploring and experimenting
- using feedback to adapt actions

- discussing what they do

- reflecting on what happens

- articulating what happens.

If learners are to be active, reflective and creative, then teachers and lecturers have to act differently. Traditional methods, built around the transmission model of education – lectures, whole-class teaching, books, videos, all presentational forms – must be supplemented by far more opportunities for learners to be active.

We must move to the next generation of e-learning products that will empower teachers and lecturers to be creative and innovative in their approach to pedagogy, able to create the opportunities for learners to optimize their learning experiences.

The e-strategy encourages this by proposing a move toward more 'flexible learning activity design tools'. We should be using the technology to make it easy for teachers and lecturers to define a sequence of learning activities, populated with their own materials (e.g. slides), or borrowed (e.g. a colleague's video) or commercial materials (e.g. a multimedia interactive game), as they have always done, but to be able to do this in a digital world, making full use of all the properties of interactive, adaptive, dynamic, communicative and collaborative environments the technology offers.

The goal of personalization should be changing how practitioners work. Staff must be sufficiently confident – they must have the right skills and they must have access to the right technology – if they are to use ICT to transform teaching and learning.

Supporting teachers and lecturers

We have to recognize the pressures that make this kind of innovation difficult. Staff often find themselves working against the grain of the organization as they try to introduce more ICT. As well as effective training, they need supportive leadership; time to experiment and refine their practice; opportunities to share ideas and experiences with other practitioners and to adapt them to their own work; and sufficient support from experts in online library skills, learning technologies and learning design.

We must enable front-line professionals – teachers, professors, tutors, library staff, classroom assistants – to make the most of technology in everyday work.

Our priority here is to build a professional workforce that can collaborate and innovate. Teachers, professors and support staff, together with their unions and professional associations, are well placed to help us discover the most effective ways of improving support for learners through ICT. We must give them the means and the motivation to achieve these end objectives.

References

DfES (2004), *Five Year Strategy for Children and Learners*, Nottingham: DfES Publications. See www.dfes.gov.uk/publications/5yearstrategy/.

DfES (2005), *Harnessing Technology: Transforming Learning and Children's Services*, Nottingham: DfES Publications. See www.dfes.gov.uk/publications/e-strategy/.

POLICY PAPERS

2

The Paradox of Choice and Personalization

Sara de Freitas

ncreased choice for the consumer is creating a need for personalized support and greater flexibility over where and how learning may take place.

Personalization: definitions and critical perspectives

The development of what Fauré, in 1972, called a 'learning society' – that is a society whose ambitions are predicated upon education and learning – has, in recent years, emerged as a key factor in the economic considerations of most modern democracies. For these often competing nations there is now a common realization that the social requirement is for a highly educated and skilled workforce capable of adapting to a post-industrial labour market and which is able to engage with the levels of informational tasking which can support what Castells, at the turn of the millennium, termed the 'network society'.

Both these ideas – the learning society, predicated upon universal education and lifelong learning, and the network society, predicated upon the rapid processing and communication of large volumes of information – are, of course, consistent with each other, not least in the tools and approaches that are common to both. At this transitional point, however, there is still an ongoing debate over the way in which education and lifelong learning should be delivered, with some notable tensions emerging between those, who favour the personalization of learning – with client-specific, tailor-made services and customized content – and those who see the educative requirements of a global network society in terms of universal disciplinary considerations and global approaches.

Driven as it is by political agenda and underpinned by consumer-driven factors, the idea of 'personalized learning', has been largely supported through reports and events organized by the Centre-Left think tank Demos and has been championed by Charles Leadbetter in his considerations of the role of personalization, in general, across the social institutions (2004a). Leadbetter argues that '"deep" personalization of education content would give users a far greater role ... promoting greater capacity for self-management and self-organization' (2004b, p. 20) – virtues which, in turn, would be promoted into the public sector, resulting, it is hoped, in better governance and innovation.

This approach, however, has been greeted with some scepticism and no little criticism, not least because the term personalization is associated with many different disciplinary perspectives. In Education the term has been used generally to mean the consumer-driven provision of personalized and individualized learning content. In the political sphere the term has become equated with a need to improve choice in the public services and institutions (Miliband, 2004). At the same time, technological approaches to the term have centred upon integrating information systems and services with individualized requirements (Dagger *et al.*, 2005). Any understanding of the term 'personalized learning' therefore has to take into consideration the educational and technological potential of personalized (filtering or recommender) learning services such as portals, virtual learning environments and customized search engines, as well as engaging with the economic and social implications of extended choice in the public sector.

However, there are some perceptions about personalization which are buoyed up by, at times, unrealistically high expectations and assumptions about what technological innovation, e-learning and blended learning can achieve in practice. This has, to some extent, already led to misconceptions about the scope of what personalization can achieve, leading to concerns from teachers, some of whom feel disenchanted about the over-hyped 'push' of relatively immature tools and technologies intended to support and supplement traditional learning and teaching practices. While new developments are beginning to support the personalization agenda to promote evolving global and personal learning practices, time is needed to embed new tools and systems into practice, and this needs to be accompanied by well-considered and historically sound pedagogic approaches (Beetham, 2005). At the same time, a more effective collaboration and interchange between communities at macro, meso and micro levels is needed: through policy, research and practice.

The 'choice-personalization paradox'

Another critical aspect to be considered is the role that increasing choice is playing in the development and evolution of learning-based systems. While convergence of technologies and tools, interoperability and standards offer us the possibility of increased ease of use for the consumer (through single entry point systems and integrated systems), increased choice for the consumer is creating a need for personalized support and greater flexibility over where and how learning may take place (Clark, 2004).

Greater choice over the mode of delivery and access to digital content is also allowing for greater possibilities regarding how content is personalized for individual needs and increased functionality (e.g. portal systems). This tendency highlights another critical trend in the development of learning practices and may come to have profound implications for how teaching and learning is conducted in years to come (Leadbetter, 2004a, b, c; Bentley and Wilsdon, 2003). The 'one-size-fits-all' approach to pedagogic delivery which has served learning communities in the past is changing in favour of more tailored and personalized approaches made possible, in part, through the development of e-learning systems and individualized approaches – student tracking, e-portfolios and personal learning plans – that guide the lifelong development of the learner, allowing for differentiated learning, online learning and face-to-face collaborative approaches (Sutherland, 2004).

Increased choice, then, is not just perceived: the Internet does offer a diverse range of access to reusable learning materials and content; however while the consumer-led drive towards greater choice does appear to offer more, the extra time associated with searching for what is needed and a continual blur between work, play and learning are putting greater strains upon available time, leading to prioritizing the range of choice rather than the quality and depth of content.

This ostensible trend is leading many teachers to favour tried and tested tools rather than risk using materials that are not tied to established curriculum objectives and outcomes.

This relates to an underlying paradox whereby the processes of digitization and the incumbent proliferation of information coupled with extending choice over modes of delivery of e-content are leading to an increased need for greater filtering processes; the more choice the greater the need for filtering. However, by definition, the greater the filtering the less control the learner may have over the content delivered thereby creating a powerful paradox that may have the opposite effect than that which was originally intended. While the idea behind personalization has broadly been to provide increased choice, higher quality content and more learner control, the net impact of this approach may paradoxically be to provide less choice, lower quality content and reduced learner control.

This qualitative shift away from the in-depth and refined approaches more associated with traditional forms of media (e.g. books, magazines and journals), is offering more choice – yes, but with less control and discretion over what is actually consumed. Choice is being offered but at the expense of depth and quality, occasioning 'demotivation' problems, and even producing cognitive overload in some cases (Schwartz, 2004). In reaction to this overload of information, any approaches that lead to time and cost efficient filtering and selection are being welcomed, and this drive in turn fits in with the general desire to *reduce* the data that we are dealing with every day.

Personalization can, however, offer a chance for reducing these multiple possibilities, by tailoring them more closely to what is required through pre-selection. Although personalization does offer a balance to indiscriminate choice, there are problems associated with how this filtering process is mediated: what is selected and what is not selected, why is one option selected over another option, and ultimately who controls that selection. Although problematic, the ambitions driving the trend seek to place more emphasis upon the learner, and this approach is, in turn, promoting the development of user-based systems. This may represent a trend for future delivery and production of learning content, with an emphasis upon learning content that may be authored by the learner or collaboratively (Davies, 2005).

Taken in this way, personalization does offer the potential of access to global learning resources through personalized portal systems that can be customized according to learner specification, thereby allowing for services and learning content to be integrated and developed in new ways. However, an entirely learner-centred approach to learning may prove elusive, as existing models of content production and delivery are based upon long established models – where teachers are the producers of learning content – and this approach would be radically altered, should future models of production be based upon the notion that learners develop their own content.

Conclusions

The current situation seems to underscore this headline tension between global priorities and localized and personal needs; a tension that is not always inherently inclusive. However, while we may argue about definitions of personalization, more concerning is the underlying paradox that more choice may actually be less, and it is essential that this underlying paradox be fully considered in relation to our shared social and learning priorities. Furthermore while we must ensure that the learner's voice is heard and that quality learning and teaching is protected in the rush to digitize our processes of learning content delivery, we must also ensure that personalized learning approaches do, in fact, improve upon established practices and bring in more, not less, learner participation and choice. In order to build a unified and collaborative vision of what personalization means to the learning community, collaborative work needs to be undertaken to bring together policy, research and practice-based perspectives, to ensure that if this is the right course to take personalizing learning will have substantial benefits to support the fast-changing challenges of the 'learning society'.

References

Beetham, H. (2005), 'Personalization in the Curriculum: A view from learning theory', in S. de Freitas and C. Yapp (eds) *Personalizing Learning in the 21st Century*, Stafford: Network Educational Press, pp. 17–24.

Bentley, T. & J. Wilsdon (eds) (2003), *The Adaptive State: Strategies for personalizing the public realm*, London: Demos.

Castells, M. (2000), *The Rise of the Network Society*, Oxford: Blackwell.

Clark, D. (2004), 'Personalisation and e-learning', Epic Group plc. See: www.epic.co.uk/content/resources/white_papers_index.htm (last accessed 6 September 2004).

Dagger, D., V. Wade & O. Conlan (2005), 'Personalization for all: Making adaptive course composition easy', in special issue of *Educational Technology & Society*, IFETS.

Davies, S. (2005), 'Personal Learning Tools and Environments: Their role in supporting the independent lifelong learner', in S. de Freitas and C. Yapp (eds) *Personalizing Learning in the 21st Century*, Stafford: Network Educational Press, pp. 63–66.

Fauré, E. (1972), *Learning to Be*, Paris: UNESCO.

Leadbetter, C. (2004a), *Personalization through Participation: a new script for public services*, London: Demos.

Leadbetter, C. (2004b), *Up the Down Escalator: why the global pessimists are wrong*, London: Penguin.

Leadbetter, C. (2004c), *Learning about Personalization: how can we put the learner at the heart of the education system?*, Nottingham: DfES Publications.

Miliband, D. (2004), 'Personalized Learning: Building a New Relationship with Schools'. See: http://www.dfes.gov.uk/speeches/speech.cfm?SpeechID=95 (last accessed 6 September 2004).

Schwartz, B. (2004), *The Paradox of Choice: why more is less*, New York: HarperCollins.

Sutherland, S. (2005), 'e-Portfolios: A personal space for learning and the learner voice', in S. de Freitas and C. Yapp (eds) *Personalizing Learning in the 21st Century*, Stafford: Network Educational Press, pp. 79–82.

3

Personalization in the Curriculum: A view from learning theory

Helen Beetham

I f all learning is personalization, we need to ask whether learning opportunities should be personalized for the learner, and if so, how this might enhance the process of personalization by the learner.

Charles Clarke, in his foreword to the DfES five-year strategy, promises: 'flexibility to help meet individual needs; and more choices between courses and types of provider, so that there really are different and personalized opportunities available' (DfES, 2005a). So central has the idea of personalization become to the Government's education strategy that in May 2004 Professor David Hargreaves was appointed by the DfES to 'clarify the concept' and recommend how it could be realized across education sectors. In the same year, personalization became a key focus of both the JISC Distributed e-Learning strand (Davies, 2005) and the Becta e-Learning Practitioners Conference.

The briefest glance at learning theory, however, suggests that learning is, by definition, personalized. Bruner and Piaget's insights, now widely accepted under the banner of constructivism (Bruner, 1990; von Glasersfeld, 1995), have been supported by 60 years of research and practical experience. Far from being passive recipients of knowledge, learners are actively involved in trying to make sense of the world around them, and of other people's constructions of it. Until it has been personalized – integrated into a personal theory or personal structure of competence – nothing new can be said to have been learned. Even traditions very different from constructivism emphasize that personalization is essential to learning. Behaviourist theories anticipate that learners will develop personal repertoires of behaviour that represent a more advanced stage of learning than mere reproduction. Theories that lean towards socially situated and supported learning, nevertheless, describe the development of personal roles, and ultimately identities, within community rules and structures of knowledge.

Perhaps the most interesting theorist of learning-as-personalization was Lev Vygotsky. The concept of internalization was at the heart of his writing about human development: 'Any capacity in children's development appears twice, or on two planes... First it appears between people as an inter-psychological category, and then within the individual child as an intra-psychological category' (Vygotsky, 1978). Knowledge that is articulated socially becomes internalized and available for private reflection. Skills that are performed with the help of social rules and mediators become internalized and available for private practice. Researchers since Vygotsky have found strong evidence for internalization (see for example Rogoff, 1990; John-Steiner, 1995; Hobson, 2002), and for another of Vygotsky's tenets: the need for internalization to be supported by 'semiotic mediation' or the use of shared tools, artefacts and signs (Hasan, 2002).

If all learning is personalization, we need to ask whether learning opportunities should be personalized for the learner, and if so, how this might enhance the process of personalization by the learner. Another of Vygotsky's well-established laws of development is that learning takes place in a 'zone of proximal development', where learners' capacities are extended beyond what they are capable of independently, but not so far that they cannot participate meaningfully in shared activities and dialogues. This suggests a first way in which learning activities could be personalized: to provide the right degree of challenge for learners' current state of development.

Vygotsky, and his collaborator Luria, were deeply interested in the differences between learners, including learners with physical disabilities. Gindis (1995) shows how their work highlighted the variety of psychological tools and mediational means (including, for example, Braille and sign language) that could be used to help learners develop. Learners differ not only in their physical needs for mediation, but in their level of cultural development or capacity to participate effectively in particular forms of exchange. Advanced learners can use a wide range of cultural tools to support their internalization process – Brown *et al.* (1993) identify books, videos and computer systems as potential mediators for learners who are able to use them in a dialogical manner. Less skilled or confident learners experience the same cultural artefacts not as tools for mediation and dialogue, but as impenetrable surfaces or, at best, alien terms to be learned by rote. A second aspect of personalization might therefore involve finding mediational means – language, tools, artefacts – that are appropriate to the learners' psychological and cultural competence.

A third aspect of personalization, closely involved with the second, involves the affective response to learning. If learning involves mediated activity, both the activity and the mediation must be experienced in a positive way. Learners must understand and share the goals of the activity, even if the processes are not yet fully mastered. They must feel included by the language and the artefacts used, and must recognize a role for themselves in the shared activities and dialogues that take place.

Throughout this discussion, learners have been left in the plural where possible, to indicate that for Vygotsky learning is a socially mediated activity in the first instance. The goal of learning is internalization, but this is not its starting point. Personalization takes place in an environment that is supportive of the individual learner, but not necessarily individualized. Personalization should not, then, be promoted at the expense of dialogue, guidance, collaborative activity and peer support. Only when learners are already skilled, and working in their own cultural comfort zone, can their learning be mediated by artefacts (resources, books, computer systems) alone. This theoretical position is strongly supported by the annual National Institute of Adult Continuing Education (NIACE) survey of adult learners (NIACE, 2004), which shows that the gap between social classes in terms of participation in adult learning has increased year on year, in parallel with the rise in computer ownership. In terms of cultural capital it is true to say: to those that have shall be given.

The remainder of this paper considers some implications of this discussion for personalization in the curriculum, particularly in a technology-rich learning environment, which provides the context for much of the personalization debate.

Access

Some learners experience physical, sensory or geographical barriers to participating in learning. Many more experience cultural barriers. The ability for learners to use their own preferred interface – from their own home or workplace if necessary – is an important step in overcoming these barriers. There is less of a cultural gradient to climb if learning is experienced in a similar way to more familiar kinds of activity such as gaming or chatting with friends. The capacity to use a personally available technology to participate in learning is clearly a significant benefit to disenfranchised learners, but access should not be confused with participation. Nor does 'user-friendliness' necessarily provide the right level of challenge to put learners in the zone for effective development of their capabilities. Access to the curriculum is a necessary but far from sufficient requirement for personalized learning.

Learning cultures and literacies

As argued previously, skilled learners can personalize the most unpromising artefacts and situations. Even a didactic textbook can be questioned, plundered, criticized and argued with. A central question for a truly personalized curriculum must therefore be: what are the skills, habits and values that characterize this kind of learner? Lea and Street's (1998) work on academic literacies indicates that the effective learner's habits of mind are complex. They include criticality, reflexivity, self-confidence, a flexible repertoire of information skills, and a questioning attitude to cultural authority (Lemke, 2000). Capacities of this kind are developed only through guided practice (APA, 2004), in authentic contexts (Greeno et al., 1996) with the support and affirmation of what Vygotsky calls 'more capable others'. They cannot be developed simply through access to resources, however carefully these may have been selected to meet learners' needs. A curriculum for personalization will devote a great deal of time to the development of these capacities, particularly within subject teaching and at transition points, recognizing that they involve positive enculturation as well as mechanistic development of skills. The Joint Information Systems Committee (JISC) has just funded an important new study into the characteristics of 'successful' e-learners, which will explore the development of learning literacies in a technology-rich learning environment (Sharpe et al., 2005).

'Flexibility and choice'

Personalization of learning can be achieved in two ways: by adapting what is offered to meet the needs of the learner and by allowing the learner to select from a range of offerings. The first of these is dealt with to a limited extent below ('Learner differences'). The second – Charles Clarke's 'flexibility and choice', or what Charles Leadbeater (2004) describes as the 'shallow personalization' of mass customization – forms the core of the government's manifest for education, as for other public services. Learners are invited to design their own pathways through ready-made units of learning, with guidance, personal development planning and e-portfolios offered to support their decision making – if they are lucky.

Again it is important to ask whether learners have the capacity to behave as well-informed consumers in this educational marketplace. Personal development planning in higher education is a closely-directed and iterative activity (EPPI, 2003), as institutions recognize that making effective choices, learning from those choices and reviewing their effectiveness, are challenging even for postgraduate and professional learners. A curriculum that promotes these skills will demand a high level of personal support, and the evidence suggests that this should be integrated into subject teaching (Hattie *et al.*, 1996), and not left solely to guidance officers and personal tutors.

Second, research is needed into what choices actually benefit learners, including choices within given units of learning, such as whether and how to engage in group work, how to demonstrate competence, the 'mediational means' used for participation and what to submit for assessment. As curricula are increasingly standardized, these choices may become less rather than more available. Sara de Freitas (2005) has described the curtailment of choice within a wider curriculum offering as the 'choice paradox'.

Finally, in line with the debate over other public services, one can question whether consumer choice is an appropriate model for education. From adult basic skills to higher learning that 'qualifies' individuals as members of a professional community, learning involves fundamental changes in a person's outlook, values, social role and personal identity. This is not an argument for making learning more difficult than it needs to be: it is an argument for recognizing learning as self-actualization and self-transcendence (Maslow, 1943), with all the difficulties that this entails. The mass customization model favours the already well-informed consumer, and fails to take into account learners' natural resistance to change. Curricula for personalization should anticipate that learners will be demoralized and self-doubting at times, and rather than steering them away from these situations should provide extra support from staff and peers, recognizing that these are often the moments when a step change in personal world-view and capability is taking place.

Learner differences

In Further Education (FE) and schools particularly, personalization is seen as an extension of a long-standing agenda for differentiation of learning to meet the different needs of individual learners. There is no doubt that valuable work has been done to meet the needs of learners with physical and sensory impairments (Doyle and Robson, 2004). There is controversy, however, over the more wholesale use of 'learning style' inventories to categorize learners as having a particular set of learning needs (Mayes, 2004). Coffield *et al.* (2004), in a comprehensive review, highlight the lack of reliable evidence that stable learning styles exist independently of the contexts in which they are expressed, and the lack of consensus about how learning and teaching ought to be organized in light of these apparent differences. Even if diagnostic tests were reliable, should learners be accommodated in their preferences, or encouraged to extend their repertoire? Should learners form working groups that bring a wide range of different styles to bear on a problem, or tackle tasks that are appropriate only to them?

At present the 'strong' vision of personalization envisages learner records being used to diagnose individual learners' needs and adapt what is offered accordingly (DfES, 2005b). This is a superficially attractive vision, sometimes described as 'just-in-time, just-for-me' learning. Apart from the cost implications of offering multiple versions of the same curriculum, however, the prioritization of individual preference over, for example, the cohesive effects of learning in a cohort, are still unproven. In line with doubt over the stability of learning 'styles', it is also doubtful whether a learner's needs and motivations can be adequately diagnosed in advance of actual participation in a learning event. This is an argument for more expert teachers, in more dynamic and responsive learning environments, not for more diagnostic tests (Northedge, 2003). Differentiation can actually undermine the role of the expert teacher, ushering in a new division of labour between those who design learning opportunities, those who deliver the version that is right for a particular learner and those who help learners choose between the offerings available. More evidence is needed that individualization offers real benefits before it is used to justify wholesale reorganization of relationships between learners, teachers and educational organizations.

Learner records are potentially empowering if they are used for personalization by rather than for learners and if learners have final authority over how their progress and achievements are recorded. Even so, records represent only one data-driven version of a learner's identity. Ecclestone (2005) points out that the 'learner needs' paradigm tends to encourage low horizons of expectation and a vulnerability or deficiency model of the learner. Learners are capable of entering into different roles and, long-term, even different identities. Perhaps – given our observations about the flexibility of the skilled learner – curricula should be designed to challenge and extend rather than simply accommodate learners' sense of who they are.

Communities of practice and enquiry

Ruth Kelly, in her foreword to the Government's e-strategy (DfES, 2005b), promises learners 'a digital space that is personalized, that remembers what the learner is interested in and suggests relevant websites, or alerts them to courses and learning opportunities that fit their needs'. In fact, the most effective 'personalized' services depend on extended communities of common interest. Rather than diagnosing an individual's requirements from their private interactions with the system, Google, Amazon, Napster, and academic information services of the kind pioneered by the JISC (Davies, 2005) use the remembered behaviours of other people to direct the user toward resources that are likely to be of interest. Other services rely even more explicitly on communal knowledge building, for example through shared favourites and lists, recommendations, peer reviews, annotations, human indexers, wikis and collaborative blogs. Again, participation in these communities demands a degree of cultural capital or information literacy to begin with, but their popularity – without any need for promotion or policy intervention – indicates how attractive personalized services can be when they are based on shared activities and interests. Research into the benefits of personalizing learning, then, should also look carefully at the benefits of shared learning in a cohort or larger community. Rather than designing individualized opportunities for their learners, colleges could be providing them with tools to organize themselves and learn from one another's interests and strengths (Lave and Wenger, 1991; Cole, 1995; Hughes, 2005).

Martin Johnson, writing in the Education Guardian (December 2004) argues that 'politicians should not be calling for the personalization of education, but rewarding the socialization of education. They should measure individual achievement less and social cohesion more.' While this is undoubtedly a political position, it is one that chimes with much currently accepted learning theory.

Personalization and empowerment

As the last quotation suggests, personalization is a questionable and contested term. Does it mean mass customization – tinkering with the means to some predetermined ends (the formalized learning outcomes of a given unit of learning) so as to make them appear more user-friendly? Does it mean personalization for the learner, carried out by some invisible other within the learning system? Or does it mean learners having a personal stake in the goals and outcomes of their learning? Does it mean personalization by learners of the situations and communities in which they learn?

Formal learning is, by definition, an accommodation of the individual to the demands of the community. What is oppressive about much formal learning in schools and colleges is that learners are disempowered within that community – they have no say over its goals and values, or means of delivery. Empowering learners to personalize their own learning means addressing them not only as well-informed consumers but as creative people with their own agendas, and as citizens of a learning democracy. It means giving them a say over how they learn and the technologies they use to do so. Personalization is a political rather than a technical project.

References

APA Education Directorate Task Force on Learner Centred Psychology (2004), *Learner Centred Psychological Principles*, American Psychological Association

Brown, A.L., D. Ash, M. Rutherford, K. Nakagawa, A. Gordon and J.L. Campione (1993), 'Distributed expertise in the classroom', in G. Salomon (ed.) *Distributed Cognitions: Psychological and educational considerations*, New York, NY: CUP, pp. 188–228.

Bruner, J. (1990), *Acts of Meaning*, Cambridge, MA: Harvard University Press.

Coffield F., D. Moseley, E. Hall and K. Ecclestone (2004), *Should We Be Using Learning Styles? What research has to say to practice*, Learning and Skills Development Agency.

Cole, M. (1995), 'Sociocultural settings: design and intervention', in J.V. Werch, P. Del Rio and A. Alvarez (eds) *Sociocultural studies of mind*, Cambridge UK: Cambridge University Press, pp. 187–214.

Davies, S. (2005), 'Personal Learning Tools and Environments: Their role in supporting the independent lifelong learner', in S. de Freitas and C. Yapp (eds) *Personalizing Learning in the 21st Century*, Stafford: Network Educational Press, pp. 63–66. See also www.jisc.ac.uk/index.cfm?name=etools.

de Freitas, S. (2005), 'The Paradox of Choice and Personalization', in S. de Freitas and C. Yapp (eds) *Personalizing Learning in the 21st Century*, Stafford: Network Educational Press pp. 13–16.

DfES (2005a), 'Five Year Strategy for Children and Learners'. See www.standards.dfes.gov.uk/innovation-unit/personalisation/fiveyearplan/?version=1.

DfES (2005b), 'Harnessing Technology: transforming learning and children's services'. See www.dfes.gov.uk/elearningstrategy/.

Doyle, C. and K. Robson (2004), *Accessible Curricula*, Cardiff: UWIC Press.

Ecclestone, K. (2005), 'Personalized Learning: lowering educational horizons or meeting learners' real needs?', paper presented to the *Discourse Power Resistance Conference*, Plymouth, UK, March 2005.

EPPI (2003), 'The Effectiveness of Personal Development Planning for Improving Student Learning'. See http://eppi.ioe.ac.uk/EPPIWebContent/reel/review_groups/EPPI/LTSN/LTSN_June03.pdf.

Gindis, B. (1995), 'The social/cultural implication of disability: Vygotsky's paradigm for special education', *Educational Psychologist*, 30(2), pp. 77–81.

Greeno, J., A. Collins and L. Resnick (1996), *Cognition and Learning: Handbook of Educational Psychology*, New York: MacMillan, pp. 15–46, cited in R. Wegerif (2002), *Thinking Skills, Technology and Learning*, Bristol: Nesta FutureLab.

Hasan, R. (2002), 'Semiotic Mediation and Mental Development in Pluralistic Societies: Some Implications for Tomorrow's Schooling', in *Learning for life in the 21st Century: sociocultural perspectives on the future of education*, Malden, MA: Blackwell, pp. 112–26.

Hattie, J.A., J. Biggs and N. Purdie (1996), 'Effects of Learning Skills Intervention on Student Learning: a meta-analysis', in *Review of Research in Education* 66, pp. 99–136.

Hobson, P. (2002) *The Cradle of Thought: Challenging the Origins of Thinking*, London: Macmillan.

Hughes, J. (2005), 'Possibilities for patchwork eportfolios: critical dialogues and reflexivity as strategic acts of interruption', paper presented to the *Discourse Power Resistance Conference*, Plymouth, UK, March 2005.

Johnson, M. (2004), 'All Together Now', in *Education Guardian,* 7 December.

John-Steiner, V. (1995), 'Cognitive Pluralism: a sociocultural approach', in *Mind, Culture, and Activity* 2(1), San Diego, CA: LCHC, pp. 2–10.

Lave, J. and E. Wenger (1991), *Situated Learning: legitimate peripheral participation.* Cambridge, UK: Cambridge University Press.

Lea, M. and B. Street (1998), 'Student Writing in Higher Education: an academic literacies approach', in *Studies in Higher Education*, 23(2), pp. 157–172.

Leadbetter, C. (2004), *Personalization through Participation: a new script for public services*, London: Demos.

Lemke, J. (2000), 'Learning Academic Language Identities: Multiple Timescales in the Social Ecology of Education', in *Language Socialization, Language Acquisition: ecological perspectives*, University of California at Berkeley.

Maslow, A.H. (1943), 'A Theory of Human Motivation', in *Psychological Review* 50, pp. 370–396. See http://psychclassics.yorku.ca/Maslow/motivation.htm.

Mayes, T. (2004), 'Learner-centred Pedagogy: individual differences between learners', report to the *Joint Information Systems Committee.*

NIACE (2004), *The NIACE Survey of Adult Participation in Learning*, National Institute of Adult Continuing Education. See www.niace.org.uk.

Northedge, A. (2003), 'Enabling participation in academic discourse', in *Teaching in Higher Education*, 8(2), pp. 169–180.

Rogoff, B. (1990), *Apprenticeship in Thinking: cognitive development in social context*, New York: Oxford University Press.

Sharpe R., G. Benfield, E. Lessner and E. DeLicco (2005), 'Scoping Study for the Pedagogy strand of the JISC e-Learning Programme', report to the JISC.

von Glasersfeld, E. (1995), 'A constructivist approach to teaching', in Steffe and Gale (eds) *Constructivism in education*, Hillsdale, NJ: Lawrence Erlbaum Associates, pp. 3–15.

Vygotsky, L. (1978), *Mind and Society*, Cambridge, MA: Harvard University Press.

4

Leadership for Personalizing Learning

John West-Burnham

Organizational success is the sum of personal success but personalization requires a fundamental shift whereby the value system of the school shifts away from organizational imperatives to personal needs.

The personalization of learning offers fundamental challenges to the prevailing orthodoxy in schools. Personalization is still a complex and elusive theory and its full implications are not fully understood. However, it is possible and legitimate to argue that personalizing learning offers a number of ways forward, ranging from a token response to a fundamental and profound reconceptualization of how schools work.

In the context of personalization, it is important to emphasize the distinctive nature of leadership. For the purposes of this discussion leadership is perceived as having a number of characteristics:

- Leadership is fundamentally concerned with change, innovation and creativity
- Leadership is a moral activity; it is concerned with the translation of principle into practice.
- Leadership is about direction and purpose.
- Leadership is rooted in effective human relationships.

It would be wrong to see leadership and management as opposite ends of a spectrum – in fact they are interdependent; they have to work in a symbiotic relationship. The introduction of personalization requires the leadership qualities defined above but also needs highly effective and efficient management.

The scale of the challenge is shown in Hargreaves' (2004) model of the imaginaries that inform the most fundamental perspective on the purpose, values and organization of schools.

Hargreaves concludes his discussion: 'Personalizing learning ... may be seen as the driver from the 19th century educational imaginary to that of the 21st century ... The evolution of educational imaginaries is now so fast that the same leaders live through the transition and have to lead and manage it. It is this that makes the leadership of personalizing learning so important and so challenging' (p. 32).

In essence the leadership of personalizing learning is about the creation of a new mindset, a new collective understanding of the nature and purpose of schools.

While it would be wrong to underestimate the practical issues of timetabling and the use of space and building capacity across the school, the real issues are cultural, social, intellectual and moral: 'There is a clear moral and educational case for pursuing this approach. A system

19th Century Educational Imaginary	21st Century Educational Imaginary
Students are prepared for a fixed station in life.	Students' identities and destinations are fluid.
Intelligence is fixed.	Intelligence is multi-dimensional.
Schools are culturally homogeneous.	Schools are culturally heterogeneous.
Schools of a type are interchangeable.	Schools of a type are diverse.
Schooling is limited for the majority.	Schooling provides personalized learning for all.
Schools have rigid and clear boundaries.	Education is life-long for every student.
Schools work on the factory model.	Education is unconstrained by time and place.
Roles are sharply defined and segregated.	Roles are blurred and overlapping.
Schools and teachers work autonomously.	Schools and educators work in complex networks.
Education is producer led.	Education is user led.

Figure 4.1: Education imaginaries (after Hargreaves, 2004, pp. 30–42)

that responds to individual pupils, by creating an education path that takes account of their needs, interests and aspirations, will not only generate excellence, it will also make a strong contribution to equity and social justice' (DfES, 2004, p. 7).

The fundamental challenge for educational leaders is to facilitate the transition from the old to the new paradigm – to create a new mind set which will then allow for the consolidation of the personalization of learning into authentic and sustainable practice.

In the context of personalization, learning-centred leadership can be said to have a number of distinctive characteristics which are most likely to bring about the necessary and appropriate change in culture:

- openness to change
- focus on the individual
- rich dialogues about learning
- modelling strategies to support learning
- high-quality personal relationships
- shared knowledge creation
- leadership underpinned by systematic management
- a culture of success.

This list is not in any order of priority; indeed these factors need to be seen in a fluid and dynamic interaction – each reinforcing the other.

Openness to change

It was argued in the introduction to this paper that one of the defining characteristics of leadership is a focus on change, innovation and creativity. This accords precisely with any model of learning-centred leadership as learning is, by definition, a process involving change.

Leaders therefore have to be comfortable with their own learning and be open to personal change. In practice this means that they both initiate and support innovation. The process has to be seen as emergent, that is, evolving through a complex series of interactions. One of the dangers in leading change is to think of it as a neat movement from one phase to another.

It is a core function of leadership to create the environment that allows the transition to take place. This is a complex and challenging process, but, as Capra (2002) argues, 'During the change process some of the old structures may fall apart, but if the supportive climate and the feedback loops in the network of communications persist, new and more meaningful structures are likely to emerge' (p. 108).

Focus on the individual

This is perhaps the most significant and the most challenging component of learning-centred leadership, as the prevailing orthodoxy in most school systems is the responsibility of educational leaders for the integrity and success of the organization. School leadership is dominated by the related concepts of improvement and effectiveness of the school. Of course, organizational success is the sum of personal success, but personalization requires a fundamental shift whereby the value system of the school shifts away from organizational imperatives to personal needs.

In many respects all schools will need to adopt the best practices of special education – the design of all structures, processes and relationships around a detailed understanding of the needs of the individual. It might well be necessary for school leaders to revisit the fundamental values and aspirations of the school. A powerful and consensual starting point for such a review might be the five components of 'Every Child Matters':

- being healthy
- staying safe
- enjoying and achieving
- making a positive contribution
- achieving economic well-being.

These principles offer a deep moral basis to personalization in that they give status and significance to three key and interdependent principles:

- education as social justice
- a focus on the well-being of every child
- securing entitlement to success and achievement.

For Sergiovanni (2005) leadership is about 'building a covenant comprising purposes and beliefs that bonds people together around common themes and that provides them with a sense of what is important, a signal of what is of value' (p. 8).

Rich dialogues about learning

The work of the learning-centred leader has to be focused on sophisticated conversations with all members of the school community about the nature of the learning process that they are engaged in. Culture is significantly determined by language, leadership is expressed through authentic dialogue and learning is, at its most fundamental, the acquisition of language.

This implies that learning-centred leaders:

- have deep knowledge about the nature of learning

- understand the variables that inform effective learning

- have skills and personal qualities to sustain authentic dialogue

- are able to translate principle into practice.

If personalization is to work, then leaders must create 'shared meanings'.

Modelling strategies to support learning

In this context, learning-centred leaders demonstrate what it means to be a learner and the key strategies in helping others to learn. There is a very high correlation between the strategies that support effective learning and the most potent leadership behaviours; that is, mentoring and facilitation. In some ways facilitation can be seen as the generic form of mentoring in that the two share the following essential characteristics:

- a focus on learning, growth and understanding

- an enabling relationship

- a balance of support and challenge

- a focus on building capacity and moving from dependence

- a balance of focus on outcomes and processes.

If leaders do not model this kind of relationship in their dealings with adults then it is unlikely that adults will feel able to work in this way with learners.

High quality personal relationships

Leadership and learning are symbiotically linked with regard to personal relationships. In most ways leadership is about relationships. Equally, effective learning relationships are rooted in high quality human interactions. By its very nature personalization will increase the number of significant personal interactions – there will not be the same opportunities to 'hide and avoid' that the large group or class offers. Personalization will succeed or fail according to the integrity of the interpersonal relationships that exist between teacher and learner, learner and learner, teacher and teacher, and leaders with everybody.

The specific interpersonal strategies appropriate to personalizing learning might include:

- counselling, mentoring and coaching

- facilitation of diverse groups

- building trust: openness, transparency and honesty

- personal and shared review and reflection

- developing confidence through enhancing skills and understanding.

These are all areas which provide a direct manifestation of the nature of leadership and where individual leaders have the opportunity to model appropriate behaviours.

Shared knowledge creation

Both personalizing learning and the creation of learning-centred schools require, as has been argued above, the creation of a new body of knowledge, conceptual maps to inform practice and new models of roles and relationships. Using the basic principle of effective design 'form follows function' it seems appropriate to argue that leadership for personalizing learning should, of itself, demonstrate effective learning and personalization. This has to be linked with the creation of new professional knowledge. Perhaps the most appropriate model for this complex process is Wenger's (1998) concept of a 'community of practice' which creates shared vocabulary, meaning and practices. It can be argued that a primary function of leadership for personalization is to create communities of practice that create the knowledge that will allow personalization to be consolidated and developed.

Leadership underpinned by systematic management

Leadership for personalization has to be rooted in the values that will facilitate the movement from schooling to personalizing learning. However, such values have to be translated into practice that has the following characteristics:

- it is genuinely inclusive

- it is rooted in equality

- it is consistent over time.

This means that personalizing learning requires a sophisticated management infrastructure that is value driven in order to ensure that the key resource variables – time, space, people and resources for learning – are deployed to optimum effect.

A culture of success

Personalizing learning is fundamentally about maximizing personal achievement. This requires leadership that is focused on creating a culture of success which is measured by a wide range of criteria. This is very much about the symbolic role of leadership in recognizing, rewarding and celebrating success in all its manifestations at every opportunity.

It does appear to be the case that schools that succeed have an explicit culture of success: high expectations, high aspirations and overt and explicit celebration of success. This is probably one of the most transformative things a leader can do and it is manifest in most aspects of human activity – sport, the military, business and even family and community life. Optimism and hope are fundamental to engagement, commitment and motivation.

For personalization to meet these expectations that it carries, leaders need to 'radiate possibilities'. It is the function of leaders to help create (in Csikszentmihalyi's terms) the possibility of flow: 'Thus the flow experience acts as a magnet for learning – this is, for developing new levels of challenges and skills. In an ideal situation, a person would be constantly growing while enjoying whatever he or she did' (p. 33).

Conclusion

This paper has argued that the introduction of personalizing learning in schools represents a leadership challenge of a significantly different order of magnitude to those which have dominated school leadership in recent years. A substantial proportion of the reforms that schools have had to respond to have been system-wide, top-down strategies, based on improving schools. There is no such authoritative hegemony for personalizing learning.

The great challenge of personalization is a shift in our perspective of what constitutes a valid and appropriate educational experience. As such it calls into question a wide range of cultural norms, professional practices and expectations, and models of effective leadership. Personalizing learning is fundamentally and profoundly a moral issue.

References

Capra, F. (2002), *The Hidden Connections*, London: HarperCollins.

Csikszentmihalyi, M. (1997), *Finding Flow*, New York, NY: Basic Books.

DfES (2004), *A National Conversation about Personalised Learning*, Nottingham: DfES Publications.

Hargreaves, D. (2004), *Personalising Learning*, London: Specialist Schools Trust.

Sergiovanni, T.J. (2005), *Strengthening the Heartbeat*, San Francisco, CA: Jossey-Bass.

Wenger, E. (1998), *Communities of Practice*, Cambridge: Cambridge University Press.

5

Personalizing Learning: ICT enabling universal access

Niel McLean

What ICT brings to the personalized learning agenda as currently described is the ability to make it achievable, manageable, sustainable: in short, deliverable.

Introduction

The debate over how ICT supports personalized learning is timely. The potential alignment of an agenda aimed at achieving individual excellence while providing equity for all, with ICT's ability to offer what the business sector calls 'mass customization', offers a significant opportunity.

This paper begins to map out how ICT can be used to support personalized learning. Rather than offer a broad menu of possible roles for ICT, it aims to identify those areas where ICT potentially offers unique opportunities to maximize impact on the personalized learning agenda. It begins by setting out the British Educational Communications Technology Agency's (Becta) understanding of the challenge offered by personalized learning, moves on to consider ICT's unique potential contributions and how they align with Becta's future vision for ICT, and concludes by offering an outline strategy for embedding ICT within the personalization agenda.

Personalizing learning and public sector reform

The policy discussion within education forms part of a wider debate about the reform of public services.

Broadly speaking, three approaches to the issue have emerged:

- increasing flexibility and responsiveness on the supply/provider side
- increasing the influence of market forces by increasing consumer choice and moving power and influence towards the demand side
- increasing participation at all levels in the design and delivery of services through real engagement with customers, professionals and stakeholders in self-actualizing systems and communities.

The educational challenge

The view of personalized learning set out by Ministers is a broad one, moving away from any narrow vision of 'individualized' learning and recognizing that much of what constitutes learning is collaborative, builds on each learner's individual needs and is appropriately paced, with challenging assessment and partnerships which extend well beyond the physical constraints of the classroom. This aspiration is new. Although an over-simplification, education policy and practice in the latter half of the twentieth century can be characterized as a competition between individualized approaches to learning, which at their worst leave learners unchallenged by low-expectations, and overly prescriptive models, which (again, at their worst) accommodate the average while failing to address many learners' needs.

The new approach (set out in 'Every Child Matters', 'Excellence and Enjoyment', 'Opportunity and Excellence' and 'Success for All') signals a realignment in policy terms away from driving up average standards to a sharper focus on realizing the potential of every individual learner.

This new emphasis presents significant challenges:

- how to shift attention onto the individual learner without losing the focus on attainment

- how to ensure that individual expectations are sufficiently challenging

- how to monitor individual progress without increasing the bureaucratic burden on teachers

- how to ensure that teachers' feedback to learners is evidence-based, timely and aimed at increasing performance

- how to ensure that the teacher's view of the child is informed by a whole-institution perspective

- how to maximize the spread in effective practice without undue prescription

- how to maximize opportunity and flexibility while ensuring affordability (A personalized learning model of flexible specialization should be flexible enough to allow learners to identify others who want the same types of flexibility – their natural communities of interest.)

- how to capitalize on learners' increasing personal access to alternative sources of learning support and information

- how to change current teaching and learning support systems (including e-learning systems), which are based on a model of prescriptive education, to systems which can effectively support the culture change and flexibilities envisaged by the adoption of personalized learning.

All of these challenges must be met against a growing need to achieve efficiencies, focus on delivery and provide value for money.

Firstly, steps have been taken to reduce the amount of time teachers spend on non-teaching tasks through initiatives such as reducing the bureaucratic burden.

Secondly, initiatives aimed at 'restructuring' the teaching workforce, will help to improve the effectiveness of the investment in teachers.

Finally, efforts to improve the use made of Management Information Systems (MIS), to automate data collection and improve interoperability and connectivity between systems will help address the ever increasing cost base disparity.

However, it will remain the case that teaching and learning will be inherently 'labour intensive' activities and the more teaching and learning are personalized, the more potential demand they will make on teachers and schools.

Properly supported and implemented, the effective use of ICT will play a key role in reconciling these potential conflicts and meeting these challenges. In particular, it may be possible to align the agenda aimed at achieving individual excellence while providing equity for all with the potential of ICT to allow what the business sector calls 'mass customization'. Becta furthermore believes that the personalization agenda will bring a much-needed focus to the application of ICT to the education process.

The increasing complexity of the available technology

Key to the role of ICT is the need to ensure that our aspirations are underpinned by a robust, reliable and sustainable infrastructure and high-quality content. Becta believes that the personalization agenda will only be effectively realized through the systematic and system wide implementation of ICT.

Growing personal access

Today's learners are more used to personal access devices than any other generation. One of the major challenges associated with the personalized learning agenda will therefore be the need to move towards delivery models that build on this increased access to information, communities and content. Learners will become more demanding and schools will be increasingly challenged to compete with the wider availability of learning support.

Connected learners

Just as devices get smaller and more personal, the connectivity networks necessary to bring learners and content together and facilitate online collaboration become not national or indeed international but truly global. The ICT infrastructure within the school will need to look outwards.

Additionally, the school system will need to allow appropriate access by external systems to facilitate remote access.

Existing MIS systems will need a significant change of focus to support the personalized learning agenda.

However, a sharper design focus on functionality needed to support personalized learning will be required, and it will need to take account of the 'holistic' educational achievements of the learner and be capable of interacting/interoperating with all the systems that hold 'prior' information on what that pupil previously achieved.

Exploiting ICT's capability to underpin personalized learning

So what can ICT contribute to this agenda? What can it do to help to make learning 'personalized'?

- It can personalize content sources and resources, allowing those appropriate to each learner's individual needs to be effectively identified, modified, used and reused.

- It can provide pathways through that content which can be personalized to the needs of each learner and easily or automatically modified to take account of progress.

- It can present a range of interfaces to the content that are appropriate to the level and ability of the individual learner.

- It can provide collaborative tools that provide new, interesting and powerful mechanisms for communication and collaboration.

- It can facilitate effective assessment and reporting tools which are flexible, adaptive, powerful, make minimal bureaucratic demands on teaching and non-teaching staff, and allow for a detailed understanding of the progress being made by individual learners and groups of learners, and within and between institutions.

- It provides flexibility in key areas such as the decision about:

  - *when and where to learn* – for example, at school itself, at home connecting to resources at the school and beyond, or at the local library using equipment and connectivity centrally provided. Work created during any of these interactions can be added to the learner's 'online portfolio', recording progression and cumulative achievements;

  - *who to learn with* – creating opportunities to collaborate not just with students in the same 'organizational' group, but to share work with parents, grandparents, learners on the other side of the world. Additionally the capability exists for the delivery of individual courses to be shared between schools, thus potentially broadening the curriculum and increasing the viability of smaller schools, or allowing 'classes' from particularly successful schools to be 'taken' by students not actually attending that school.

In summary, what ICT brings to the personalized learning agenda as currently described is the ability to make it achievable, manageable, sustainable: in short, deliverable.

It must also be recognized that while ICT can currently bring much to the personalized learning agenda, it has a considerable distance to travel before its potential to do so can be fully realized.

Becta's vision of education supported by ICT

Becta has been working to develop a vision for the educational use of ICT that, it believes, recognizes the potential offered by ICT set out above and aligns closely with the move towards personalized learning.

For learners, ICT:

- Enhances new and existing approaches to learning, motivating learners by engaging them with their own learning, matching experiences to their needs and allowing them to drive their learning at their own pace – *engaged learners*.

- Supports individual interaction and collaboration between learners – *interactive learners*.

- Provides all learners, irrespective of their personal circumstances, with access to learning where and when they need it, specialist support and provision beyond their immediate contexts and makes learning seamless by providing continuity between learning experiences – *supported learners*.

- Allows learners to demonstrate and record their achievements in a variety of ways, recognizing both their own and others' needs – *recognized learners*.

For the educational workforce, ICT:

- Supports more efficient and effective teaching, administration and management, allowing the workforce to identify and respond flexibly to need – *an effective workforce*.

- Provides new opportunities for the educational workforce to support teaching and learning, and extend its roles and influence beyond existing institutional barriers – *an out-reaching workforce*.

- Provides access to continuing professional development, linking learners, teachers and other members of the educational workforce through communities of professional practice – *a networked workforce*.

For educational institutions, ICT:

- Improves the ways in which institutions carry out their business by supporting new institutional models and processes and allowing them to draw on external support to complement their provision – *effective institutions*.

- Breaks down existing barriers between institutions, the communities they serve, phases of education, and 'formal' and 'informal' learning – *networked institutions*.

- Extends their offerings beyond the traditional limits of time, geography and culture – *extended institutions*.

For the educational system as a whole, ICT:

- Ensures that innovation and effective practice spread throughout the system – *an innovative system*.

- Captures and communicates information on the system's performance, allowing intelligent accountability, where the locality both informs and influences the centre, and the centre adds value to the locality – *a high-performing system.*

Concluding remarks

The personalized learning agenda will only achieve its aims if it is clearly communicated to and shared with schools. The 'noise and clutter' of competing initiatives must be addressed and the agenda channelled through organizing systems such as the national strategies.

Finally, ICT should not be seen as a cheap option or indeed always as an effective option. There is a consistent danger with ICT that too much is claimed in terms of its potential impact without understanding the scale of change or the investment that is needed to achieve the required added value. Bringing together the personalized learning agenda and the ICT programme provides a real opportunity to examine and maximize the impact of both.

6

Aimhigher: Widening participation to higher education and personalized learning

Graeme Atherton

The focus on individual learners' needs here illustrates the clear connection between personalized learning and widening participation.

Introduction

Widening participation to higher education has been a professed target of the present government since the turn of the century. It is embodied in the well known 2001 target outlined by the then Education Secretary that, by 2010, 50 per cent of young people aged 18–30 should have an experience of higher education. The White Paper on Higher Education in 2003 was explicit regarding the need to target young people from lower social class groups (DfES, 2003). In particular, access to higher education reached new heights of political sensitivity in 2004 with the introduction of new student funding arrangements in England.

This paper will examine the relationship between widening participation to higher education and personalized learning. In particular it will consider how ICT can support personalized learning in the context of the 'Aimhigher' project. Aimhigher, the national outreach widening participation project for England, began in 2001. It focuses on the support and development of cross-sector educational activity involving higher education, colleges and schools focused on young people in lower social class groups, from particular ethnic groups and those with disabilities.

This paper will argue that Aimhigher is using information technology to promote personalized learning. It will highlight several examples of work involving innovative use of information technology that could potentially support young people in the Aimhigher target groups by supporting personalized learning for them. It will argue that widening participation work, and specifically partnership-based cross-sector work, provides a context in which the relationship between personalized learning and ICT can be explored.

Access to higher education in the UK

Despite the increases in qualification levels across the population in the UK in the latter half of the twentieth century, as in Europe, the gap between those accessing higher education from higher and lower social class groups has remained approximately the same (Higher Education Funding Council for England (HEFCE), 2001; Segundo, 2001). In the UK, from 1960 to the year 2000, the gap between the skilled (manual), partly skilled and unskilled, and those from managerial positions in terms of attendance at higher education has widened from 25 per cent to 30 per cent (DfES, 2003).

The reasons for these differences are, on the surface, well known: cultural practices 'unfriendly' to higher education, fear of financial costs, underdeveloped routes to higher education for those pursuing vocational qualifications and in particular low educational attainment among certain social groups (Archer et al., 2003). However, what is less clear is how for individual young people these factors interact to lead to non-participation in higher education. The focus on individual learners' needs here illustrates the clear connection between personalized learning and widening participation.

Aimhigher

Aimhigher is based on local and regional partnerships of higher education institutions, schools and further education colleges. It supports a wide range of 'outreach' activities targeted at young people from backgrounds under-represented in higher education, in particular extra tuition, summer schools, contact with higher education students, information, and awareness raising events for teachers, academics and parents.

Despite considerable investment in Aimhigher, over £250 million since 2001, the government's commitment to Aimhigher has been uneven. It has suffered considerably from repeated reorganization, and its piecemeal growth has hindered its ability to forge a clear identity. The project has recently been extended from 2006 to 2008. However, funding has been reduced and increased autonomy for school and higher education institutions through the 'New relationship with schools' (DfES, 2005), which gives headteachers more control over school budgets, and changes in student funding arrangements (OFFA, 2004), which give Higher Education Institutions significant extra funds to spend on outreach work, have placed partnership working under new strains.

Aimhigher and personalized learning

The personalized learning agenda emphasizes the extension of choice for young people in their educational careers. As the 2004 DfES paper 'A National Conversation about Personalized Learning' states: 'Personalized learning demands a curriculum entitlement and choice that delivers a breadth of study, personal relevance and flexible learning pathways through the education system.'

Personalized learning, with its emphasis on choice, appears to have its antecedents in third way politics, for a long time the driver of New Labour policy. As Giddens (1998) argued, the third way is really about empowering people, including young people, to make choices. It is through choice that Aimhigher and personalized learning come together. Aimhigher is about empowering young people from under-represented groups to make an effective choice about entering higher education. For reasons of attainment, aspiration and knowledge, such young people have seldom had a real 'choice' about their educational futures: their background made the choices for them. It is through its emphasis on partnership that Aimhigher aims to 'personalize' learning for young people and move beyond barriers based on background. Partnership is important because it can offer young people choice via contact with a range of higher education institutions in a range of educational contexts. There is a large amount of outreach activity aimed at widening participation that is driven by individual institutions, but inevitably this has a degree of institutional motivation and does not offer the potential to personalize learning which is required to address the individualized interaction of barriers to higher education described above.

Aimhigher, personalized learning and ICT

There are a number of examples of how information technology is helping Aimhigher personalize learning for young people from under-represented backgrounds.

Computer gaming and simulation: UniAid and 'All About U'

The charitable foundation UniAid is presently developing an interactive computer game 'All About U', which allows young people to live and study as a first-year undergraduate student (www.uniaid.org). It gives them the opportunity to make decisions regarding how to spend money, divide their time between study and leisure, and so on and outlines the consequences of their actions. Central London Aimhigher is helping UniAid to develop teaching materials to support the game. All About U allows individual young people to identify their own challenges and their own strategies for dealing with the challenges of higher education.

Support for negotiating course/subject choice

Several Aimhigher partnerships have developed interactive online tools to allow learners, particularly those wishing to follow vocational routes to higher education, to access information about the options open to them (Action on Access 2005). There is a dearth of learner friendly information for young people in vocational areas of study. By utilizing ICT, Aimhigher is constructing the flexible learning pathways identified in the DfES paper mentioned above.

e-Mentoring

Mentoring relationships between school pupils/further education students and higher education students allow the personal needs of young people to be identified and supported. It is the embodiment of personalized learning. Aimhigher, in partnership with the charitable foundation the Brightside Trust, has initiated electronic mentoring in the medical sciences which allows online communication to extend the ability and scope that mentoring has, for example, to overcome distance boundaries and manage time pressures of mentors and mentees (www.thebrightsidetrust.org). ICT personalizes learning by making mentoring more flexible and individualized.

New challenges for Aimhigher, personalized learning and ICT

Firstly, changes in student funding arrangements with increased tuition fees and differentiation across Higher Education Institutions (HEI) in student support arrangement mean that, increasingly, the cost of attending higher education is individual to the learner dependent on location, course, institution and their own labour market skills. The challenge is how ICT (and initiatives like All About U and online information tools outlined above) can be used to deliver user friendly, impartial information to allow learners from under-represented backgrounds to make informed choices here and not be put off from engaging with higher education choices by the complexity of the scenario.

Secondly, widening participation does not mean just accessing HE for widening participation students; it means surviving and prospering when they are there. The differences between Level 3 drop-out and higher education are significant and contribute to the problem of student attrition. Personalized learning may contribute to the problem if it is understood differently in different sectors. The challenge is how information technology can support communication across sectors through virtual learning environments, and so on, which prevent this happening. Aimhigher as a partnership initiative may be able to contribute here.

Conclusion

This paper has argued that the concept of personalized learning has some foundation in choice and empowerment and has outlined examples of it being made real through using information technology in the context of Aimhigher. However, the concept is in need of further development and exploration. How far is it a descriptive term for existing good practice in Aimhigher and other contexts, rather than a driving principle? How does personalization relate to partnership? Are the two principles in conflict or mutually dependent? Aimhigher provides a working context for exploring these questions and, in particular, the influence that information technology can have on this developing policy agenda.

References

Action on Access (2005), *Progression to HE from WBL and work related learning*, Bradford: Action on Access.

Archer, L., M. Hutchings, C. Leathwood and A. Ross (2003), 'Widening participation in higher education – Implications for policy and practice', in L. Archer, M. Hutchings and A. Ross (2003), *Higher Education and Social Class: issues of exclusion and inclusion*, London: Routledge Falmer.

DfES (2003), *The future of higher education*, Nottingham: DfES Publications.

DfES (2004), *A National Conversation about Personalised Learning*, Nottingham: DfES Publications.

DfES (2005), *A new relationship with schools: the next steps*, Nottingham: DfES & OFSTED Publications.

Giddens, A. (1998), *The Third Way: The renewal of social democracy*, London: Polity Press.

HEFCE (2001), *University Participation of 18–20 year olds*, Bristol: HEFCE.

Office for Fair Access (2004), *Producing Access Agreements: OFFA Guidance for Institutions*, Bristol: OFFA.

Segundo, S.N. (2001), 'Access in the OECD: the unfinished business of the 20th Century', in L. Thomas and M. Cooper (2001), *Access to Higher Education: The Unfinished Business*, Stoke on Trent: Trentham Books.

7

Workforce Reform and Personalized Learning

Chris Yapp

I believe that we have to look beyond the teacher–pupil interaction and look at all the roles needed within a system of learning.

My central hypothesis is that learning has always been and always will be a personal experience. A decade ago when I first wrote and spoke about this I used to talk about individualized learning and I found that term to be very divisive, whereas personalized learning has been treated more empathetically by the teaching profession. Individualized tended to give the impression of replacing teachers with computers and pumping instruction into empty vessels through automated pedagogies. The argument for my central hypothesis is that learning is at its heart a social and a socializing process. So what is new now?

I would argue that it is the organization of education itself that is impersonal. By this I mean that the reliance on mass curricula, high-stakes testing, rigid timetabling and so on detracts from this personal experience rather than supports it. Good teaching and learning practice can compensate for this 'institutionalization' of learning and frequently does. The problem for society as a whole is that personalized learning has in the past not been economically scalable and sustainable. As part of the educated elite – Boys Grammar and Oxford – I have myself experienced one-to-one tutorials and benefited from that interaction.

The growth of the internet and the world wide web has made, and will continue to make, access to the world of knowledge increasingly easy. So technology offers the prospect of lowering the barriers that have prevented some personalization of the experience of education to the 'many not the few' as the PM Tony Blair would describe it. Governments are rightly concerned over universality of access and social equity. We are increasingly in a position in the UK where access to technology is rising at home and at school and college, so policies to tackle the digital divide can ameliorate the problems faced by groups at risk of exclusion.

When we have tackled the access problem, all I would argue is that we have created an environment for individualized not personalized learning. It is in principle, for me, no different to giving every family in the UK free books or encyclopaedias. I can think of few who would argue that this would be sufficient to tackle the educational divide in the UK.

The central challenge I believe then is to understand how we might take advantage of technological progress to create new institutional forms and working practices that allow us progressively to scale a system of personalized learning, underpinned by increasingly universal access to the world of knowledge.

For me, we can learn a lot by looking at the organizational forms developed to support 'on demand' behaviours such as 'lot size of one', just-in-time in manufacturing. What is important is to understand that much of the systemic thinking in this space pre-dates the computer revolution, but technological advances have allowed this approach to be globally scalable and integrated across complex supply chains.

What then should be the characteristics of a system of 'learning on demand' that we might evolve over the next generation? I argue that we have to think of this as a timescale of 20–30 years to abstract ourselves away from a technocratic vision of education, or a focus on the short-term access issues, to concentrate on the necessary social innovations required to realize the promise of personalization for all.

First, we have to acknowledge that new pupils are not new learners. As Howard Gardner (1991) reminds us in *The Unschooled Mind*, what children learn before starting school is quite amazing. The role of parents as first teachers of the child is increasingly recognized in child care policy for instance.

Second, children learn through play. Learning is an active and participative activity, not passive absorption of facts and ideas. Prof. Stephen Heppell is a personal hero of mine, as I know he is of many others in this field. When I get the world-weary question, 'isn't lifelong learning a life sentence for many?', I use him as an exemplar of the change in ethos that I think is central. Stephen is one of the most child-like people I have ever met. He is constantly buzzing with new ideas, new stories, new games and new friends in a way that we find mostly in a children's playground. Because he is a grown up we call it 'research', but the truth is that it's about learning through play, which is why he is such an engaging speaker and colleague. Pat Kane's (2004) book *The Play Ethic* provides an interesting critique of the protestant work ethic. The idea that a 'knowledge society' is a 'playful society' is appealing to me personally, but also highly contentious. The role of gaming technology in learning and the arguments about 'dumbing down' are testament to the raw nerve such ideas touch.

Third, good teaching makes a difference. The role of teachers will change, I believe, dramatically over the next generation, but this will create new levels of expertise. The notion that teachers are moving from the 'sage on the stage to a guide on the side', has been around more than a decade. I find this observation unhelpful. My own experience is that good teachers are a mix of both. The balance may well shift, but the observation does not capture the richness of the interactions that need to be understood if the potential benefits of workforce reform are to be fully achieved.

Fourth, there is an inherent tension in education between the transmission of the best from generation to generation and preparing young minds for a world we do not yet know or comprehend. When I describe the systemic model as 'learning on demand', there is a need for expansion here. My argument is that we are seeking a balance in a system of education and training that helps the learner to fulfil their own potential. Over-simplistically, education is best just-in-case, while training is best just-in-time. While the access infrastructures for a new 'paradigm' of learning can be created by sustained investment, the interactions between curriculum, assessment and pedagogy need to evolve together and funding is necessary but not sufficient. This is probably the hardest aspect of change management I foresee and is my rationale for believing that this is a generational programme.

Finally, personalization of assessment is the key to unblocking the limits of existing provision. As parents, if our child is doing grade 8 piano while doing grade 2 violin we tend to be quite proud not sad. Yet in mainstream education we are supposed to believe that our child should be level x at age y in all subjects. It seems to me that for both teachers and learners the straight jacket of summative assessment causes more resentment than any other aspect of existing provision. However, confidence in a new system by teachers, learners, parents and employers is vital. Creating an environment of testing at 'stage not age' has long been discussed. Comparisons with the driving test are frequently used.

If these are the characteristics of the system required to support personalized outcomes, how and where do we start?

Alec Reid some years ago described to me his vision of transformed education as a society where young people put on their 'L plates' to say 'I am a learner', rather than took them off to say 'I have passed'. I find this an elegant starting point as well as a goal.

I would argue that we need to start by redefining teachers as learners. Once we do that, we can think about how to support a personalized system of learning for the teaching profession so that they become masters and role models of learners rather than 'merely' subject experts.

This I believe has major ramifications for teacher recruitment, development and retention. I have characterized elsewhere teaching as being the loneliest profession. A model which has one teacher and x learners puts a heavy burden on the teacher. Looking at the organization of 'on demand' systems, what is clear is that the efficiency and effectiveness of such organizations requires a move to greater team working rather than a simple focus on individual performance. In the Open University we have a good example of an innovation a generation ago where curricula of high quality were, and are, produced by a new organizational form, of teams rather than individual academics.

It is this move to team-based teaching that I believe allows for the evolution of pedagogy in step with curriculum and assessment. How is this to be achieved? My own view is that the starting point needs to be in formative assessment. If we change the question from 'how good a teacher are you?' to 'in what way are you a good teacher?' we can analyse a richer set of teaching roles which can be combined to allow for the development of a set of new professionals and paraprofessionals which can underpin a scalable system.

This is why I believe that we have to look beyond the teacher-pupil interaction and look at all the roles needed within a system of learning. When I describe teachers as learners, obviously subject expertise remains important. In a world where knowledge is increasingly available in vast amounts, we need 'teachers as researchers'. It will become an important goal for teachers to maintain their own expertise in a chosen field. In turn, librarianship or curatorship – the ability to organize information and knowledge to be able to build and share with others – is necessary to create a learning context. The ability to structure learning environments and content puts a premium on authorship. On top of this, mentoring and counselling skills are required to optimize interventions in the support of learning. The ability to assess, and in particular self-assess, to reflect on one's own learning and learning needs, is then critical.

The challenge today is that teachers try 'individually' to fulfil all these roles. Rather than a work overload, I would argue that today's professionals suffer from a role overload. I am not claiming to have all the answers. However, I strongly believe that we need a debate about the full set of roles and team-based 'supply-side' organization if we are to create a world-class system of learning fit for the twenty-first century.

I want to go one step further. One problem I believe that we suffer from today is that there is a mismatch between a widespread agreement of the need for 'confident independent learners' alongside a system that many claim, under pressure to improve results, increases dependency of the learners. Around 1992, I remember Sir Christopher Ball arguing that the ideal teacher–pupil ratio was twice the child's age. At age 1, two parents is ideal; at age 5, ten to one; at age 10, twenty to one; and so on. Much of the evidence that I have seen shows that social equity in educational attainment is best delivered by early interventions. For me, the argument has a lot of merit. It may be that this kind of resource planning is what will be needed to combine high standards, equity and independent learners.

I hope that what I have argued for here is clear. The journey to personalization for all learners has to start with personalized learning for the teaching professions. Models of team work and new organizational forms will create the capacity for scale and sustainability, but these will take time. My examples I give to stimulate debate rather than as a complete solution. Learning is after all, at best, work in progress.

References

Gardner, H. (1991), *The Unschooled Mind: How Children Think and How Schools Should Teach*, New York, NY: Basic Books.

Kane, P. (2004), *The Play Ethic: A Manifesto for a Different Way of Living*, Basingstoke and Oxford: Macmillan.

PRACTICE PAPERS

8

Personalized Learning: Personalized schooling

Derek Wise

I f teachers are to find the time and space in a classroom setting to use a personalized approach, technology can come to their aid.

It is 7am and John wakes up to the sound of his hi-fi playing his favourite track through his Philips Streamium wireless media box, which accesses the music stored downstairs on the living room computer. Wiping the sleep from his eyes, John studies his face in his dressing table mirror, which, at the press of a button, doubles as a computer screen and television. A red laser light marks out the letters of a computer keyboard on the dressing table surface and infra red sensors work out what John is typing. John uses the computer to turn on the central heating and his shower. Once downstairs he orders the food for his sixteenth birthday over the internet via the 'kitchen shopper', which reads John's scribbled notes from his tablet PC.[1]

Once out of the house John catches the bus to Humdrum High School where he is in the final year of studying for his GCSEs. At Humdrum High all the lessons are 50 or 100 minutes long whatever the subject and the vast majority take place in egg box like classrooms. Knowledge is centred on both the teacher and the curriculum. John is dependent on others in terms of what should be learned, how it should be learned, where it should be learned and the pace and conditions of learning.

Contrast John's control over his home environment with school where the control over time, place, power space and pace reside elsewhere. We don't need terms like 'personalized learning' to tell us we need to change our schools. It's obvious that they are in danger of becoming an anachronism. However, personalized learning or personalization is useful because it points the way forward. All across the public services, particularly health and social care, personalization is the rallying call for change. And it's about time we started to take it seriously in education.

If you ask the students, they will soon tell you that whether we like it or not we are in charge of institutions. Comparisons of school experience in France, Denmark and England found that English children enjoyed school and lessons the least, were most likely to want to leave as soon as they could and felt that the school got in the way of their lives. Writing to the Guardian newspaper in 2000, a student commented that he no longer wished to be treated like 'herds of identical animals waiting to be civilized before we are let loose on the world'. Others compared schools to 'giant magnolia prisons'. It was clear what they did want: light, colourful classrooms; a school that listened to them and where their opinions mattered; a school without a rigid timetable, without a one-size-fits-all curriculum; and a school where they could learn through

---

1   Every piece of technology mentioned here is available as this book goes to press. See the article 'House of the Future Today', *Daily Telegraph*, 22 April 2005.

experience, experiments and exploration, including going outside to learn. One way of summing up all of this is to conclude that they wanted schools to become more personalized, a 'home from home'. So it's clear that we need, at least as far as our students are concerned, to make schooling less institutionalized. Instead of fitting an individual student into a system – twentieth-century thinking – we need to create a system designed around the needs, aspirations and interests of individual students.

But what of personalized learning? What does that mean? Clearly, it must embrace the concept of anytime, anyplace, anywhere learning. A not unreasonable concept in our 24/7 society. It should also embrace the concept of 'just-in-time learning' – what you need, when you need it. I think, however, that at its core, personalized learning means creating independent learners. This means developing in our students the skills, attitudes and dispositions that they need in order to learn well, whatever the conditions and without the help of a teacher. As Alvin Toffler perceptively said, the illiterates of the twenty-first century will be those who don't know how to learn, unlearn and re-learn.

So what does all of this mean in practice? If our teachers are to personalize their teaching in the classroom, they will need to have a much deeper appreciation of learning styles than is currently the case. There has been too much focus on visual, auditory and kinesthetic (VAK) and Multiple Intelligences and insufficient consideration of the work of other theorists such as Kathleen Butler and Strong, Thomas, Perini and Silver in the United States. These colleagues link students' learning styles to specific teaching strategies. For example, in their article in *Educational Leadership* (February 2004) Strong, Thomas, Perini and Silver identify a Learning Styles Inventory for maths and link this to favoured teaching strategies (Figure 8.1). They wisely suggest ways of using this information in practice.

Learning Styles Inventory: Maths	
Style	**Favoured classroom strategies**
Mastery Style – step-by-step working	Step-by-step demonstration and repetitive practice
Understanding Style – searches for patterns, categories, reasons	Needs emphasis on concepts and the reasoning behind mathematical operations
Interpersonal Style – learns through conversation, personal relationships and association	Co-operative learning, real-life contexts and applications
Self-expressive Style – visualises and creates images and pursues multiple strategies	Likes visualisation and exploration, investigation

Figure 8.1: Learning Styles Inventory

We generally develop preferences and strengths in one or two of these. We need to develop all four. If a student is struggling or needs an extra challenge however, we can personalize their learning, e.g. a student with a penchant for creativity and imagination was challenged to create a metaphor, he chose digestion, to internalize the operation solving process. (Strong et al., 2004)

This is a rich vein for future research. The best advocates for learning style analysis have always been cautious in its use. Barbara Prashnig from New Zealand suggests, for example, that knowledge of individual learning styles should be used when introducing a new and difficult concept. Another fruitful line of enquiry would be to personalize homework by allowing students to present their understanding of their work using their preferred teaming style.

If teachers are to find the time and space in a classroom setting to use a personalized approach, technology can come to their aid. In my own school, lessons are collectively and collaboratively planned and put onto the intranet, so they are instantly available together with their associated resources via the interactive whiteboard. We employ our own web designers to aid this process and we use an early finish on Wednesday afternoons – students go home at 2pm while staff stay working in departments or training until 4.15pm – to create the time for collaboration. Freed from having to plan in detail a lesson and collect together the associated resources, teachers are encouraged to focus on personalizing the lesson using a detailed knowledge of the students and the way they learn. Targeted questioning and intervention personalizes the experience for the student.

We also use the timetable in a flexible way to cater for individual needs and interests. For six weeks of the year we reconfigure timetable time to enable departments to have their students for whole days or half days. This leads to a new type of learning and an opportunity for students to start something and see it through to the end without the process being interrupted every 50 to 100 minutes.

Changing the time variable eases the way to change the 'place' variable. Already 25 per cent of our Year 10 works off campus and there are growing opportunities for students to individually negotiate working from home on specially designed learning modules. In this scenario the school becomes the hub of learning, the 'broker' of learning opportunities. Through negotiation with the student and their family we help to determine where the best learning opportunities exist for the young person to achieve his or her goals. Surely catering for individual learning styles, changing the time and place for learning and through negotiation opening up a rich choice in a 'school without walls' is the essence of personalized learning? Well, no. Important though it is, I believe we need to go further and provide students with the skills, habits, dispositions and attitudes they will need to continue learning throughout their lives.

Schools are very good at helping students learn more and therefore raise achievement. We are good at direct and explicit instruction, chunking the syllabus for them, providing revision classes and so on. We are also increasingly good at helping our students to learn better by allowing students to discover their individual learning styles and taking this into account when we teach by giving opportunities for co-operative and collaborative learning. But we have to go further and help our students become better learners by teaching them how they learn and therefore how to become more effective and independent learners. This will involve giving our students the opportunities to practise and refine metacognition strategies and to specifically develop the keys to effective learning, which at Cramlington we call the 5Rs (see Figure 8.2), developed from the work of Alistair Smith.[2]

---

2   Alistair Smith's new *Learning to Learn* course, partly written by teachers at Cramlington Community High School, is available from www.alite.co.uk.

Developing a **responsible** learner

Developing a **resilient** learner

Developing a **resourceful** learner

Developing a **reflective** learner

Developing a **reasoning** learner

Figure 8.2: The 5Rs

It will involve our students in more enquiry-based work and project work. Here students will have more control over the pace of their learning. Already our AS level and A level students spend 20 per cent of their time in each subject studying independently on assignments and projects set by their teachers. We need to stop talking about the percentage of teaching time and start talking about the percentage of learning time.

Hand in hand with personalized learning we need to personalize the whole school environment. We must start treating our students as we would expect to be treated as adults (Figure 8.3).

? Do your students have social areas in which they can unwind?

? Do your students have supervised cloakrooms where they can leave their coats and bags?

? Would you use the toilets the school provides for the students?

? Are the toilets 'bully free' zones?

? Do your provide your students with a confidential, personalized counselling service?

Figure 8.3: Treated like adults?

We need to look at the way we organize our schools so that they feel more personal to our students. This could include, for example: house systems with vertical tutor groups replacing year systems; the creation of 'schools within schools', either through separate self-contained blocks housing upper/lower school students, or creating career schools/interest schools for Years 10 and 11. Here, for example, all students taking a particular career pathway would be grouped together in their own mini-school and their Maths and English courses would, through choice of topic, content and methodology, be relevant to their vocational interest.

Above all we need to change learning environments. Too much money is being wasted on impressive facades and shopping-mall type style schools which impress the public and please architects but do little to enhance the learning. We need to look specifically at the learning spaces within our schools, and this doesn't just mean the size but also the furniture and equipment within those learning spaces. At Cramlington, for example, we created out of an old social block a twenty-first-century learning environment consisting of three double size teaching rooms with a large central 'breakout' area. We designed round tables for our rooms to house a 'home team' of four students. Each table has a desktop computer for collaborative work and underneath each table four networked laptops for individual work.

The room is sufficiently large for the centre to be used for whole-class teaching or circle time. The room is carpeted and painted in 'cool blue'. It feels spacious, doesn't look anything like a computer room even though it bristles with IT equipment, it is light and airy and, oh yes, the students love it. We did this internal design on our own without any architects involved, hiring our own furniture makers to create what we wanted based on our analysis of the learning needs of our students and our desire to create independent learners.

The last thing we want is for the Government, or indeed anyone else, to come up with a definition of personalized learning. It is a concept that is inspiring and potentially transformative. I have used this article to briefly explore what I think it means for my school. There are many other important features of personalization that space precludes me from exploring. You will have different and quite possibly more innovative ideas.

Ultimately, my philosophy and why we have enthusiastically embraced personalization is summed up by my favourite educational quotation: 'What we need is a metamorphosis in education. From the cocoon a butterfly should emerge. Improvement only gives us a faster caterpillar' (Banathy, 1995).

References

Banathy, B.H. (1995), in P.M. Jenlink (ed.) *Systematic Change: Touchstones for the Future School*, Palatine, Illinois: IRI/Skylighting, Training and Publishing Inc.

Strong, R.W., E. Thomas, M.J. Perini and H.F. Silver (2004), 'Creating a Differentiated Mathematics Classroom', *Educational Leadership*, 61(5), Alexandria, VA: ASCD.

9

Personalized Learning in Practice: Challenges, approaches and ICT

Bob Banks

Schooling young people to have genuine power in shaping their own learning environment could have radical benefits for our society.

The basic premise of personalization – that everyone is different and has different needs – is not new to teachers. However, there are significant logistical difficulties in tailoring learning experiences to personal needs with limited resources. ICT tools (Banks, 2004; McLean, 2005) and other new approaches can help, but it is also important to learn from past experience and current practice.

This paper is informed by the experience of teaching in a school which took the personalization agenda a long way (Watts, 1977), including:

- learner voice being a core part of decision making

- negotiated personal learning programmes for all students

- negotiated project work, rather than whole-class teaching, at the heart of the learning process

- awards and modes of assessment selected to give best possible fit to a personalized curriculum

- learners expected to interact with the wider world – going out into the community for parts of their learning

- learner support, primarily through teachers working together as a team.

We reflect on some of the key challenges that arose for teachers in practice, and suggest ways of addressing those issues, both in general and through ICT. Although the discussion is grounded in the school sector, it does have relevance across all sectors.

Managing resources and choreographing activities

When three learners finish their activities simultaneously, or get stuck, are the resources to engage them in the next activity to hand? Will learners experience 'death by worksheet'? Is there the right mixture of inspirational adult input, engaging activity, reflection, discussion, and group work? Just as there are many pupils who find the whole-class teaching approach demotivating and difficult, so there will be pupils who find alternative 'personalized' approaches problematic; are they catered for?

Resource management is a core skill for this style of teaching. Systems for sharing and reusing resources, and a culture of sharing and co-development are very important. Also, a variety of approaches and inputs are needed. This may include group work and whole-class work and input from 'experts' from the community, from fellow students and from 'visiting teachers'. Also, students may go out into the community – 'melting the walls' of the school.

ICT can make resources more accessible, potentially automating what comes next through virtual learning environments (VLEs). It can also help teachers to find, share and reuse resources – for example through resource repositories – and to choreograph and share sequences of learning – through learning activity management systems. Interactive online resources can greatly expand the types of activity available. Online connectivity can make wider resources (people, organizations, and so on) outside the school more accessible, and person description protocols, such as 'Friend of a Friend' (FOAF) can help with this. Mobile devices can support learners in their learning and help keep their focus while they are learning in the community.

Supporting personal learning pathways

Where has each learner reached, and where are they going next? Is the next learning activity for a learner actually the most appropriate to their level of understanding and preferences? Or is it just the most obvious or convenient one 'to hand'? Is there the right balance between what others may feel each learner 'needs' to learn and what the learner feels he or she wants to learn right now? Do learning pathways add up to an overall learning which is coherent and comprehensive, and which maximizes learners' chances of good awards?

Clear record-keeping, in one format or another, is an essential skill for teachers in a personalized environment. Embedded ways of assessing what the learner has learned, and what they need to learn next, are helpful. However, teacher input is also essential, including setting a pace for each learner that is appropriately challenging and avoids 'drift'. Organizational structures whereby teachers get to know 'their' students well are important. Building up learner engagement in assessing their own progress and developing their own individual learning plans (ILPs) will also help.

It is important that awards and modes of assessment fit a personalized curriculum well. Such awards are not thick on the ground, but more are being developed and piloted. (Some examples include Ultralab's Certificate of Digital Creativity (Moss, 2005), the GCSE in Medionics (Ulicsak, 2004), Edexcel's English and English Studies GCSE.) Many, though not all, involve a significant amount of summative e-assessment, whether through e-portfolios or e-tests.

ICT can also help with diagnostics and formative e-assessment, sometimes suggesting the next learning activities based on the outcomes. This can take the form of 'adaptive' virtual learning environments, but it is important that the learner (and the teacher) is in control, and that the ICT is a guide, not a dictator. Helping to track learner progress and achievement, flagging up 'drift' and other problems, is a widely recognized role for VLEs and other ICT systems. e-Portfolios and online ILPs can support learners managing their own learning and staying focused on their goals, while sharing their ideas, where appropriate, with their teachers and peers.

Working with problematic behaviour

This is always going to be an issue in any school: indeed any community. Student empowerment and autonomy is part of the solution, rather than part of the problem. Nevertheless, in moving to a more open, personalized setting, different problems will arise, and a strategy is needed to address these.

The overall culture of the school is crucial. Broad support from all participants (students, staff, parents, and so on) is important. If students genuinely have a voice in the school and strong ownership of their own learning programmes, this also helps. Pods or teams, where close relationships between students and teachers are fostered, can also make a real difference.

ICT can help through virtual/managed learning environments where all students' learning pathways are accessible online – so that negotiations in problem situations can start from an uncontested baseline of the student's pathway. Parents' portals can make all partners aware of behavioural issues and help when working together on them. Good ICT activities can be highly motivating in themselves, and the empowerment that comes with self-ownership of learning can help defuse problematic situations.

Fostering a team approach to learner support

This is needed where learning is centred on the individual learner, rather than subject specialisms.

Team support helps with many of the challenges, but requires investment and skills and the right culture to make it work. In the new approach to integrated children's services, and 'extended schools' (Teachernet, 2005), this should extend beyond the schools to professionals working with children in social services, health, and so on.

ICT can support sharing of information and dialogue where the team members are not in the same place at the same time. It can also make team processes and decisions explicit, so less open to misunderstanding.

Managed learning environments (MLEs), integrated children's systems (DfES 2005a), e-portfolios, online ILPs and personal portals are particularly relevant technologies.

Giving genuine voice to learners

Schooling young people to have genuine power in shaping their own learning environment could have radical benefits for our society. However, it is far from easy. It requires a significant culture change and development of new skills for teachers and learners.

ICT, though by no means central, can help with equalizing different learners' voices, making inputs transparent and accessible to all, supporting consensus building, reflection and group action planning. Technologies such as group e-portfolios and online discussion forums are relevant.

The approaches for meeting these challenges clearly relate to the 'five components of personalized learning' proposed by the Department for Education and Skills (DfES, 2005b). These are:

- assessment for learning (relating particularly to 'personal learning pathways')

- effective teaching and learning (relating to all the challenges)

- curriculum entitlement and choice (relating particularly to 'personal learning pathways')

- organizing the school (relating particularly to 'team approach to learner support', to 'learner voice' and to 'working with problematic behaviour')

- beyond the classroom (relating particularly to 'managing resources' and to 'team approach to learner support').

The challenges and approaches suggested here are by no means definitive. However, an initial attempt at laying them out seems important for moving beyond theory, to actually implementing personalized learning in a widespread way.

References

Banks, B. (2004), 'Personalized Learning: Making the Vision a Reality with ICT', www.tribaltechnology.co.uk/html/company/papers.htm.

DfES (2005a), 'Integrated Children's System', www.dfes.gov.uk/integratedchildrenssystem/.

DfES (2005b), 'The five components of personalised learning', www.standards.dfes.gov.uk/personalisedlearning/five/.

McLean, N. (2005), 'Personalizing Learning: ICT enabling universal access', in S. de Freitas and C. Yapp (eds), *Personalizing Learning in the 21st Century*, Stafford: Network Educational Press, pp. 31–36.

Moss, M. (2005), 'Personalized Learning: A failure to collaborate?', in S. de Freitas and C. Yapp (eds), *Personalizing Learning in the 21st Century*, Stafford: Network Educational Press, pp. 67–71.

Teachernet (2005), 'Extended Schools', www.teachernet.gov.uk/wholeschool/extendedschools.

Ulicsak, M. (2004), 'Medionics at Leasowes Community College', www.nestafuturelab.org/viewpoint/art29.htm.

Watts, J. (ed.) (1977), *The Countesthorpe Experience*, London: George Allen and Unwin.

10

Knowledge and Skills for Individuals: A tiered approach

Rob Arntsen and Tom Holland

The practical problem of designing personalized learning spaces, applied to a real-world skills deficit, complicates the binary opposition between traditional tutor-led design and emergent personalized learning.

Background

In recent years, a theoretical model has emerged in e-learning that sets up a binary opposition between 'vertical' and 'horizontal' models of the field. It is usually put something like this: e-learning has shifted from a model where knowledge is transmitted down to the pupil according to a curriculum that is predetermined by a tutor or subject-matter expert – the 'traditional', vertical model – to a model where learners are given the space to organize their own learning content – the 'emergent', horizontal model (Powell, 2005; Serraga, 2004).

This binary approach gives us a useful position from which to approach the challenge of designing a knowledge and skills delivery system for individuals – with a focus on their personal needs – as opposed to the traditional VLE approach, where the design is approached from the viewpoint of the training delivery team.

In this paper, we'll look at the example of e-learning environments designed for individuals working in smaller businesses in the retail sector. We'll explore how the practical problem of designing personalized learning spaces, applied to a real-world skills deficit, complicates the binary opposition between traditional tutor-led design and emergent personalized learning. Building on this example, we wish to propose a tiered approach to the design of knowledge delivery systems, that enables users to organize their learning with the support and guidance of experts, employers and tools such as a Skill Gap Analysis (SGA) system.

Designing a knowledge delivery system for individuals: the context

The nature of retail raises particular problems for the provision of knowledge and skills development to the sector. Smaller retailers are usually those with the least available resources (financial and human) to spare, yet they are most in need of new knowledge and skills. Recent research suggests that to survive and compete, small retailers need to learn of new developments in the sector and acquire the skills to adapt their retail offer, modes of delivery and levels of service (MMU, 2000).

Despite the urgent need for knowledge and skills, it is estimated that 20 per cent of people in the retail sector have no qualifications and 12 per cent have an NVQ Level 1 as their highest qualification. This is associated with low levels of employer engagement with qualifications (DNTO Retail, 2000).

This lack of engagement with traditional 'vertical' modes of teaching would seem to make the sector an ideal test-case for a learning model which, tailored to the needs of the individual, promises to be more flexible and engaging.

However, there are obvious risks associated with the move away from traditional VLE design where knowledge is transmitted down to the 'pupil'. Personalized learning systems that give the learner control over content seem to provide an ideal opportunity to engage 'hard to reach' constituencies like the retail sector. But it is also true that the extra labour required on the learner's part – who is now responsible for organizing as well as following through – is a potential obstacle.

In the case of small retailers who have been disengaged from traditional qualifications, the burden of time was as important a reason for their disengagement as a perceived lack of training needs. ('Most of the kids we have,' one panellist commented during the development-phase consultation, 'need a lot of training which we never have time to do.') This was particularly true of the time burden associated with what they saw as less essential supporting activities. 'We haven't got time to sit down and look out the programs that will be useful to us,' another panellist said. 'You have to show us.' So there was a danger that learners would see personalization as costly in terms of time.

Solutions that promise to empower users as the main creators of content often focus on the opportunities afforded by the arrival of large numbers of learners with a high level of technical expertise (Serraga, 2004). Our previous work in this area, MyKnowledgeMap for Managers, used the analogy of a computer filesystem to enable learners to build personal learning libraries from an enormous number of management resources.

However, such approaches run the risk of ignoring the needs of learners with fewer ICT skills. A model of personalization accessible to retailers would put less emphasis on models of content creation only familiar to technically experienced learners.

The ability of the system to tailor learning provision to the specialist demands of the workplace, and to deliver learning that had a visible impact on the store's bottom line would be essential to the system's success.

And on a broader level, the widespread adoption of personalized learning systems can be seen as presenting a political challenge.

The idea of a 'digital space that is personalized, that remembers what the learner is interested in and… alerts them to courses and learning opportunities that fit their needs' has recently received the endorsement of the Secretary of State for Education and Skills (DfES, 2005), but the adoption of a universal model of citizens' e-portfolios requires political will.

Any solution that hoped to address the problems outlined above had to be sensitive and adaptable to the need for wider public adoption beyond the area they were originally designed to address.

Beyond the binary model

If we look at the development of e-learning practice over the last 15 years, things appear slightly different from this binary model of 'vertical' and 'horizontal' learning. Rather than a tectonic shift, what we actually see is a gradual development.

Above, we've discussed a binary opposition between:

- traditional instruction, based around the agenda of a training delivery team (not amenable to customization or personalization – e.g. CD-ROM)

- an emergent model based around the needs of the learner (highly amenable to personalization).

Let's add to these a third position: consider the kind of VLE in common use today – based around the agenda of the training team, not amenable to personalization, but highly customizable, according to, say, a learner's role in their organization, or the course their team leader deems appropriate.

What this suggests is that we aren't looking at a field divided by the stark binary opposition between training delivery team on the one hand and learner on the other. Rather, many parties have an interest in supporting the learner's development at many levels – experts, employers and peers, for example.

For the retail knowledge and skills delivery system, we looked at how their input could be used to support the learner in building a personal learning plan. The solution we proposed involved developing a tiered profiling system.

The solution

The final system offered a learning and skills delivery infrastructure designed by experts. But it was very different from a traditional 'vertical' model, where knowledge is handed down as a 'given' to the pupil.

The structure was divided into various tiers; in each tier, the delivery is tailored to the needs of the individual, either by the employer, by the learner with guidance from a Skill Gap Analysis self-assessment system (which allows them to prioritize their learning according to what they themselves see as important to their job-role) or, finally, by the unguided learner.

The completed tiered system can be schematized like this:

Expert tier

The overarching structure of the system represents an 'expert tier' – subject matter experts and instructional designers create a framework in which employers and learners co-operate to build a personal learning plan.

The large number of learning materials themselves, covering a wide area of retail topics, are created by subject matter experts in consultation with retailers. They are then organized by employers and learners according to profiling in the employer and personal tiers.

There is scope for a tutor or person responsible for delivery to customize learning materials at detailed content level: text within the e-learning objects can be edited, and content can be 'plugged in' to expand the scope of a course.

Employer tier

The employer sets an overall training policy, profiling the knowledge and skills that will be required according to job roles in their business.

The employer can then fine-tune each person's access to learning objects to ensure that learning is relevant to a particular individual, as well as job role.

Personal tier – definition

The individual reflects on their learning priorities and goals with the help of a skills self-assessment component. In the case of the Retail Detail system, the Skill Gap Analysis was itself capable of being personalized – and this local area of personalization, too, followed the tier structure:

- An employer tier, where the employer can set priorities by job role.

- An individual tier, which allows learners to fine-tune their own settings according to their own skill targets and levels of priority before they begin assessing their skills.

- The SGA suggests learning opportunities related to an individual's own skill gaps and allows them to build their own learning plan from the suggested learning objects.

Personal tier – reflection and refinement

People have the ability to override the default settings for their job roles to cater for specialist situations.

Finally, once individuals have built their own learning plan, they have the facility to keep track of their learning using their own personal e-portfolio.

We believe that this tiered approach, guiding learners toward a personalized learning plan with guidance from experts (who set the defaults for what is accessible by the various job-roles, and for the SGA system), employers (who profile individuals by assigning individuals to a particular job role and tweaking their default settings) and the learners themselves (who build a personal learning plan from available learning with guidance from the SGA) addresses the problems outlined above.

It divides the work of personalization between interested parties, so that no one tier will present an insurmountable time burden; it is simple to use for learners who don't have advanced ICT skills; and it involves the employer, while giving the learner ultimate control over their personal learning experience. What is more, it uses a framework that is scalable and that can be applied to other learning scenarios.

References

DNTO Retail (2000), *Skills Foresight Report,* Harpenden.

DfES (2005), *Harnessing Technology: Transforming Learning and Children's Services,* Nottingham: DfES Publications.

Manchester Metropolitan University (2000), *Towards a Healthy High Street: Training the independent retailer,* Manchester.

Powell, S. (2005), 'Choice, Personalization and Learning'. See http://blog.ultralab.net/~stephenp/blog/archives/001156.html.

Serraga, D. (2004), 'Creating, sharing and reusing e-learning content', position paper. See http://europa.eu.int/comm/education/programmes/elearning/doc/workshops/elearning%20content/position%20papers/segarra_david_en.pdf.

11

Personal Learning Tools and Environments: Their role in supporting the independent lifelong learner

Sarah Davies

An important aspect of lifelong, cross-institutional learning is the learner's ability to pull together, demonstrate and reflect on skills and knowledge built up through many routes.

This paper outlines the concept of distributed e-learning as it has grown through the JISC (www.jisc.ac.uk) Distributed e-Learning Programme and looks at the way in which personal – rather than personalized – learning tools and environments can support this.

Our working definition of distributed e-learning is the effective use of technology to assist learners to access, piece together and manage the learning they do throughout their life, in a range of institutional, informal and work-based settings. It is a recognition that learners – or people – engage in a wide range of formal and informal learning throughout their life, perhaps being involved with more than one setting or institution concurrently. Where e-learning is used as part of their study, they are often currently required to use a system such as a VLE which belongs to the institution concerned, which will often be different from other systems they may have used on other courses, and which will store a very limited view of the learner which only takes into account his or her activities on one particular course. This leads to a number of practical issues such as the need for multiple log-ins, the need to learn different interfaces, and the difficulty of exporting data such as contacts or a bibliography from one system to another. Learners are expected to interact with these services in different contexts and on different machines, perhaps using different operating systems and a range of media for storage. In this situation, learning becomes fragmented and it is difficult for learners to be able to reflect and build upon their skills and achievements.

Personal learning environments offer a potential way to address this issue. These are owned and managed by the learner and allow learners to carry out a wide range of learning-related tasks in their own environment, whichever course or institution the tasks are associated with. Personal learning environments (PLEs) contrast with institutionally-provided learning environments such as traditional VLEs: even if the latter can be personalized in line with user preferences, they still provide an institutionally-centred view of learners and their activities and usually only support study at a given institution. PLEs could be envisaged as portals or as desktop environments and could also be tailored to fit the needs of mobile devices. Clearly, these environments would have to be able to interact with institutional systems and with systems in use by other learners, to allow the exchange of various sorts of data. The e-Framework for Education and Research[1] (formerly the e-Learning Framework),

---

1   See www.e-framework.org for further information.

developed initially by JISC and the Australian Department of Education, Science and Training (DEST), sets out a blueprint for how this interaction of client applications and service providers could work, based on a service-oriented approach. If institutions, for example, can expose functions such as formative assessments through a web service interface, students can carry these out in their own preferred environment, perhaps submitting them back to a tutor to facilitate support and maintain a progress report. This approach relies on the use of defined web service interfaces for various groups of functions, such as assessment, e-portfolio, messaging and search. It also relies on the use of standard data formats. We are just about to begin a project within the Distributed e-learning programme which will explore the concept of the personal learning environment further and will surface many of the challenges and opportunities of this approach.

An example of a step towards the personal learning environment can be seen in the University of Birmingham's Interactive Logbook (www.il.bham.ac.uk). Although this application is delivered within a single institutional context, it offers much of the functionality that would be expected of a PLE. The Interactive Logbook was initially designed by a team of six third-year students as part of a Masters of Engineering degree, and development was taken forward by Birmingham's Centre for Educational Technology and Distance Learning (CETADL), with funding from JISC. The software developed for the Logbook provides a personal learning environment to run on mobile computers, such as a Tablet PC. The Logbook offers access to information services, collaborative tools and personal documents such as timetables and diaries in one integrated suite of tools and facilitates communication, sharing and reflection. A wide number of plug-ins are provided, such as clients for email, personal development planning, chat and personal organization, and the open architecture used allows additional software to be added as required. As well as the obvious convenience of being able to carry out tasks in a wide range of settings, owing to the use of the Tablet PC, an advantage of the system that has emerged in student evaluations is that students believe that having an integrated suite of tools makes them more efficient learners.

In order to put in place the building blocks of flexible personal learning environments, JISC has funded the development of a wide range of personal e-learning tools (see www.jisc.ac.uk/elearning_tools_home.html). Most of these tools offer a web services interface so that they can be integrated with or interact with other tools and environments within the e-Framework approach. In some cases the tools were developed from scratch during the funded period; others built a web services interface onto existing tools or prototypes. Tools developed include those for personal development planning, annotation of web pages and presentations, structured chat, assessment, mobile blogging and collaborative work. These tools are all freely available from SourceForge (http://sourceforge.net), an open source to the academic community. A second round of projects has been funded to explore the usability and pedagogical applications of some of the tools.

An important aspect of lifelong, cross-institutional learning is the learner's ability to pull together, demonstrate and reflect on skills and knowledge built up through many routes. One of the functions of electronic portfolios (e-portfolios) is to support this kind of activity. However, the usability of e-portfolios in lifelong learning relies, to a large extent, on the learner being able to either use the same personal system across different learning providers or being able to transfer key files and reflections from one system to another throughout their life. The ability of the learner to control who sees which pieces of evidence within a portfolio is important in any setting, but becomes even more crucial if a learner uses the same system for reflections on different types of learning, skills and aspirations, including those developed through or relevant to work. Reflections for personal development may be very different from those for an annual performance review, and the learner/employee would need to be confident that a manager would only be able to see those parts to which he or she wanted to grant access.

JISC-funded projects[2] have been investigating a number of issues around the use of e-portfolios and personal development planning to support lifelong learning. Particular focuses include the use of personal development planning to support students around transitions from one institution or environment to another, the transfer of personal data and reflections from one stage of education to another, such as school-college-university, and the use of portfolios to raise confidence and aspirations and potentially to help people to move back into education. The projects are helping to surface a broad view of user requirements, both those of learners in various situations, and those of the people who support them, assess their portfolios and provide administrative support. A recently-funded project is working to explore these user requirements and develop a reference model within the e-Framework which supports these requirements, showing which services are needed and how these need to fit together. This will help to develop a blueprint for a flexible set of e-portfolio components which can be combined within a personal learning environment in a way that is appropriate for the learner.

Although the e-Framework is at a relatively early stage, work is being carried out at a number of levels, from 'nuts and bolts' web service toolkits into single-institution demonstrator projects, and then through to multi-institutional pilots. These distributed e-learning regional pilot projects[3] are funded for a year from April 2005 to explore how personal e-learning tools and technologies based on open standards can be applied across a number of institutions within a region to support the lifelong learner. These projects will deliver important lessons both on the capabilities of the technology and on how well this approach meets the needs of learners, teachers and institutions.

---

2   Under the MLEs for Lifelong Learning Programme (www.jisc.ac.uk/index.cfm?name=programme_mle_lifelong2) and the Distributed e-learning regional pilots (www.jisc.ac.uk/pilotsdetail.html).
3   See www.jisc.ac.uk/pilotsdetail.html.

12

Personalized Learning: A failure to collaborate?

Malcolm Moss

I t is the teacher/lecturer who can be either a prime mover or the source of greatest inertia in any move to change the culture of learning.

Personalized learning could suggest images of the individual alone and seeking information from a distant source or a machine. Personalized learning should be delightful learning, enhanced by collaboration and assessment for learning (formative assessment).

Personalized learning should be 'personal' to the learner and meet their individual aspirations, interests and learning needs.

This position paper draws upon a variety of approaches, piloted in past and current Ultralab research projects, where the focus has been on using technology to encourage the individual to take responsibility for their own learning and, in so doing, making that learning delightful. Our research, in identifying critical challenges, has shown the importance of a clear purpose, user-friendly technology, collaboration and true assessment for learning.

It is clear that there is a need for significant change in the way we engage in learning and teaching if the personalized agenda is to be achieved.

How personal can it get? The following projects that Ultralab has piloted suggest the answer is: very personal. All involve collaboration and assessment for learning. All view ICT as central to learning and assessment and not as a bolt-on.

NotSchool (www.notschool.net)

NotSchool was created to re-engage hundreds of young people of school age back into learning and is specifically aimed at those for whom traditional alternatives have been exhausted.

All of the NotSchool researchers are provided with an Apple Mac computer, printer and internet connection at home, with access to other equipment such as a digital camera, scanner, graphics tablet, and technical support. They operate within a secure online community of learners, teachers and experts to collaborate and create their own e-portfolio. Although work can be set, produced and assessed online, the central idea is that it is not at all like school. The learners are called 'researchers' and their teachers are 'mentors'. There are also subject 'experts', 'buddies' (undergraduate or post graduate students who offer support) and 'governors', prominent people who did not get on well at school. The researchers have moved from *excluded* to *exclusive*.

In addition to personal support and formative dialogue and using a range of media, NotSchool researchers have personalized accreditation, often using unique assessment components for each researcher to match their interests or choice of media and to recognize their individual abilities. Despite their very difficult circumstances 98 per cent gain GCSE level accreditation. Some are embarking on degrees.

eVIVA (www.eviva.tv)[1]

The eVIVA project run by Ultralab and commissioned by the Qualifications and Curriculum Authority (QCA) exploited the mobile phone for both the text and voice annotation of work by peers and teachers. It was one of the tools, along with the personal computer, supporting a crucial formative and collaborative dialogue.

The eVIVA project involved Key Stage 3 students compiling online portfolios of their ICT work to evidence what they know and can do, the processes they have used and the decisions they have made. Annotating their work gave them an opportunity to show their thinking about their learning. This enables teachers to make a fairer assessment of capability. Parents, teachers and other students then gave feedback online or using a mobile or landline phone. The students had previously set their own baseline in consultation with the teacher. Once students have completed their portfolio, they have a unique oral assessment – the Viva – which they can take on any phone. The assessment can be done in a place and in a way that best suits the individual and in a way that removes exam hall stress, opening the door to greater expression and freedoms. The greater understanding of the assessment task shown by the children in the project has had a positive impact on the levels of attainment. Throughout the eVIVA process the teachers and students were much more focused on the learning taking place. As with NotSchool, eVIVA places the students at the heart of their own learning.

Ultraversity (www.ultraversity.net)

Ultraversity is a completely online degree course developed by Ultralab, where the undergraduate researchers use action research methods to explore change and improvement, both for themselves and for their workplace. Using individual learning plans and independent learning modules they identify their own learning targets. Formative dialogue in online communities with other researchers, experts and facilitators combines with the use of a variety of innovative online technologies to make Ultraversity a unique learning experience. It is collaborative, formative and personal learning.

The International Certificate in Digital Creativity

The International Certificate in Digital Creativity (ICDC), developed by Ultralab, concentrates on accrediting the creative and not the atomized assessment points of a rigid checklist. Rigour is not confused with conformity. The teacher/facilitator adopts a guided but holistic viewpoint when assessing so that no two students' work need be the same. The students may have used

---

1   The report on the eVIVA project can be accessed at www.qca.org.uk/7278.html.

entirely different techniques yet satisfied the assessment criteria. This approach requires continual collaborative support and the development of the teacher as facilitator. Informed and collaborative professionals can operate a quality assurance model; potentially relieving them of the bureaucratic burden of quality control with its constant check points and justifications.

Not the 'tyranny of the tick'

The experience of Ultralab in piloting NotSchool, eVIVA, Ultraversity and the ICDC illustrates how new technologies need not be bolt-ons to traditional practice. New technologies should not be viewed as discrete machines but as interchangeable means, capable of having a significant and positive impact in the support of personalization. These learning projects all provide evidence in support of truly embedded technology as an integral part of the learning process. It is a learning process that brings immediacy in capturing data, thoughts, notes, dialogue and images, whether still or moving. There is immediacy and simplicity in depositing that data in an e-portfolio where it can be displayed, analysed and made available to peers, facilitators and mentors.

The above projects show that assessment for learning is an essential feature of personalized learning and it need not mean the tyranny of the tick box. Assessment for learning is a term widely misinterpreted and misunderstood, but the Assessment Reform group defined it in 1999 as:

- the provision of effective feedback to students

- the active involvement of students in their own learning

- adjusting teaching to take account of the results of assessment

- a recognition of the profound influence that assessment has on the motivation and self-esteem of students, both of which are crucial influences on learning

- the need for students to be able to assess themselves and understand how to improve.

NotSchool, eVIVA, Ultraversity and the ICDC by their very way of operating, fully address all the above criteria.

While not underestimating the difficulties, all of these projects focused on the need to bring about a cultural change. Meaningful peer collaboration, the teacher as facilitator, the use of formative dialogue and the acceptance and integration of delightful technologies are all part of that cultural change. Together they can mean the successful personalization of learning and assessment. However, it is the teacher/lecturer who can be either a prime mover or the source of greatest inertia in any move to change the culture of learning.

> *Teachers will not take up attractive sounding ideas, albeit based on extensive research, if these are presented as general principles which leave entirely to them the task of translating them into everyday practice – their classroom lives are too busy and too fragile for this to be possible for all but an outstanding few. What they need is a variety of living examples of implementation, by teachers with whom they can identify and from whom they can both derive conviction and confidence that they can do better, and see concrete examples of what doing better means in practice. (Black and Wiliam, 1998)*

Personalization of the learning experience requires the careful implementation of a range of approaches, systems and technologies, but most importantly it requires a sensitive, informed and well-supported teacher ready to accept and explore assessment for learning methods. Not every teacher is ready to implement personalized learning, but purpose and motivation could be improved if teachers' involvement could, in itself, be part of an assessment for learning programme leading to say 'Investors in Learning' (Hargreaves, 2005) status.

If we fuse some of the elements described above into a coherent or cognate structure the cultural change we are seeking may be enabled in a dynamic and supportive framework that may look something like this:

- an online community with the assessment process as its purpose and centred on the students' e-portfolios

- assessment for learning incorporated into the formal assessment process

- the opportunity for the e-portfolios to be media rich, thus encouraging diverse, multimodal evidence of achievement

- the involvement of the awarding body in direct dialogue with the teacher and the learner, with moderation for fully e-assessed programmes taking place online, as evidenced by NotSchool, ICDC, eVIVA and Ultraversity

- teachers working collaboratively with other teachers in self-selecting clusters, with links to other supportive bodies and all part of an online network capable of sharing expertise, good practice and ideas.

Conclusion

Ultralab is confident of the power of online communities. Between 2000 and 2003 an Ultralab team created and developed the online communities that later formed the National College for School Leadership's online provision. These communities, regardless of geography, sector and time, enabled collaboration as serving heads shared ideas, communicated with decision makers and provided support for colleagues under pressure. This comment is typical:

> *How useful online communities are for headteachers? – combating stress; being totally up-to-date on all issues by having links to a range of web-sites ... local issues being addressed immediately; reduction of paperwork; collation of policies ... For those of us sold on the idea, there can be no going back.* (A headteacher in the 'Talking Heads' online community, NCSL, 2003)

As outlined above, Ultralab has imaginatively explored the use of ICT in the support of learning, not as a bolt-on to existing practice, but as a revolution. New technologies and online communities have the potential to place personalized learning and assessment for learning at the heart of the education system. It is important that the focus remains fixed on people, supporting, reassuring and providing motivation for both the learner and teacher in the search for delightful learning.

References

Hargreaves, D. (2005), 'About Learning', report of the Learning Working Group, London: Demos.

Black, P.J. and D. Wiliam (1998), 'Assessment and Classroom Learning', *Assessment in Education* 5(1), pp. 7–74.

13

Online Learning: Can communities of practice deliver personalization in learning?

Tim Bilham

The location of learning within communities of practice not only provides a familiar and appropriate context but also captures new knowledge and records good practice that might otherwise not be disseminated and eventually be lost to the community.

Introduction

Traditionally distance and e-learning have been driven by models where efficiencies have been won by delivering identical content and experiences to many learners. Furthermore, distance learners studied, and many still study, individualistically, frequently in isolation, while providers often have exaggeratedly promoted 'personalization' in the guise of flexibility: study at your own pace, at the time and place of your choosing. Indeed, many of the ways education is portrayed generally assume that learning is done by individuals (Smith, 2003), and much of it on their own, in private study outside of the classroom and sometimes, unfortunately, within it. Furthermore much e-learning is based upon a model of knowledge transmission, a predetermined quantum of information transferred from an expert, again often an individual, to a recipient. Personalization, or rather learner choice, is limited to an opportunity to select from the predetermined body of content often by 'fast-forwarding' through known material. Programme structures and especially assessment requirements and the need for accreditation frequently provide a significant constraint to choice. Consequently, personalization of learning is evident in only a very few online programmes. This paper focuses upon lifelong learning, in particular professional development within healthcare. It argues that personalization may be more instrumental for lifelong learning and considers how the new generation of online learning environments used in support of models of situated and collaborative learning might deliver real choice and personalization for learners.

Communities of practice

The proposition that learning is social and involves a deepening process of experience of participation in daily activities (Lave and Wenger, 1991) is fundamentally incorporated into much current educational thinking and practice. Such collective learning through social engagement is seen to result in practices that address both knowledge and social engagement and 'these practices are thus the property of a kind of community created over time by the sustained pursuit of a shared enterprise. It makes sense, therefore, to call these kinds of communities *communities of practice*' (Wenger, 1998).

Lave and Wenger's model of situated learning involves a process of engagement within such a 'community of practice' where participation is 'at first legitimately peripheral but that increases gradually in engagement and complexity'. This is an 'apprenticeship' model that allows time and space for the growth of competence and confidence. A similar model underpins many ideas for the support of learners through scaffolding (Hogan and Pressley, 1998) and has been extended to online learning by the five-stage model of engagement (Salmon, 2004) which takes learners from stage one – access and motivation – via socialization, information exchange and knowledge construction to the fifth stage of development. At this final stage learners have become responsible for their own learning and that of their learning community. They can develop the ideas acquired through online activities and apply them to their own contexts. In this way they are able to personalize their learning.

For newcomers to a community of practice, Lave and Wenger's proposition is that, 'the purpose is not to learn *from* talk as a substitute for legitimate peripheral participation; it is to learn *to* talk as a key to legitimate peripheral participation'. This is key to a discussion of whether personalization is for the learner or by the learner and whether structures such as curricula and assessment inhibit full personalization. The former implying the guiding hand of the 'expert' and a more explicit structure, the latter an opportunity for the learner to tailor a learning experience to suit personal needs.

Salmon's model is frequently explicitly used in the process of induction to online learning, to the consolidation of discursive activities within programmes and to the development of high order skills. Over time, such collaborative learning develops practices within the community and builds the knowledge base effectively. Thus personalization can also become a way of helping validate new practice and share good practice.

Building knowledge

Knowledge transmission models rarely recognize that the learners have a valuable and real personal contribution to make, and traditional designs and delivery mechanisms militate against participation. Yet learners, especially lifelong learners, have enormous experience that is too infrequently shared within learning programmes. Adult learners all have experiential stories to tell, case studies to relate, critical incidences to analyse and good practice to share and as a result are an invaluable and underused resource for learning programmes. Through their participation these communities of learners provide contextual significance, relevance and opportunities for comparative analysis that bring a richness to the learning that frequently cannot be obtained through conventional means, often because of resource limitations. Lifelong learners bring experience, context and a focus upon real-world solutions, and they are often, especially professionals, members of informal or formal communities of practice. As a result, personalization of learning appears to have more immediate applicability to lifelong learners.

It was Tennant (1997) who argued that 'new knowledge and learning are properly conceived as being located in communities of practice' and this contextualization of learning not only becomes the sine qua non of being a modern professional but it also reflects and supports the prevailing cultures within professional life, including healthcare. Professional life contains many communities of practice, including in the NHS (Urquhart *et al.*, 2002), where working and learning in inter-professional teams are commonplace but current e-learning methodologies rarely provide support. The new generation of online learning environments not only capture these contributions efficiently, but they provide the means to build a persistent archive or digital library that provides a community memory.

What is self-evident is that to deliver such objectives requires increased attention to the pedagogic design of online programmes and the need to look to digital technologies and e-tools that are both supportive of learning design and non-intrusive to the learner.

Digital solutions?

In 2002, Diana Laurillard observed that 'we have begun at last to play with digital technologies as a way of meeting the demands of the digital age, but with an approach still born of the transmission model'.

Since then, technologically supported solutions have appeared frequently and are often structured solutions in which knowledge exchange in communities of practice is achieved successfully through, for example, a personalized knowledge map (Novak and Wurst, 2003) or personalized portals (see Banks, 2004). Others promote innovation through adaptive e-learning tools, for example collaborative information environments providing community memories for supporting innovation (Stahl, 2005). Many solutions are technology-driven, and many fail to address adequately the need for placing the learner as the active agent in the learning process.

However, some newly emerging virtual learning environments (VLEs) now not only offer an opportunity to support communities of practice but also the possibility of personalizing learning by focusing on the process of learning rather than the delivery of content. There are many good examples, including those from the UK Open University. At the University of Bath, the School for Health is exploring models of learning design using a social constructivist perspective in order to promote participation among learners and with practitioners in the community of practice. Many VLEs facilitate activity-driven learning, but the open-source Moodle environment was selected because its design is based upon, and best supports, the construction of knowledge by a community and it has an educational philosophy most suited to the needs of the School's learners. The resulting programmes, launched in 2005, integrate the development of online communities of practice using asynchronous activity-driven discussion, supported by e-moderators, with learning needs analysis and personal development planning, supported by mentors, and driven by reflection on practice. Newer and experimental approaches using voice-on-line technologies will add to the blend of syndicated feeds, access to third-party resources and constructed knowledge. There are programmes for both uni-professional groups (e.g. doctors) and multi-professional groups (e.g. those working in mental health or healthcare informatics). The diversity of the group brings another dimension to the consideration of the extent to which personalization can be offered efficaciously.

Developments in these areas are at an early stage and so it is too early to draw firm conclusions at present. However, early results indicate an enthusiastic acceptance by the great majority of learners and, although most of their previous experiences have been predominantly within a knowledge transmission model, there is an intensely eager participation in collaborative activity. However the 'buy-in' from the professional and academic faculty is more mixed, a few finding it hard to reconcile themselves with new roles to do with process and support. Although much of clinical medical education has been traditionally based upon an 'apprentice-ship' role it has been located within a transmission context and for some faculty staff it does not sit as well with the model used by Wenger. Evidently there are significant organizational change issues and crucially staff development that must accompany the introduction of new learning methods. The creation of an online 'community of tutors' as part of the development is designed to allow enthusiastic faculty to draw in more traditional colleagues and is already showing signs of success. Furthermore, there is some indication that personalization of learning is evident in faculty staff as well as learners.

Summary

Personalized learning is not about individualistic learning but is a social process. Thus the location of learning within communities of practice not only provides a familiar and appropriate context but also captures new knowledge and records good practice that might otherwise not be disseminated and eventually be lost to the community. Online learning environments can now facilitate the creation and maintenance of effective and personalized learning within communities of practice, and there is a growing number of good examples of such programmes. The success of these programmes is critically dependent upon thorough attention to the pedagogic design and to a supportive programme of staff development.

References

Banks, B. (2004), 'Personalized Learning: making the vision a reality with ICT', www.tribaltechnology.co.uk/pdfs/papers/Personalised_Learning_R1104.pdf.

Hogan, K. and M. Pressley (eds) (1998), *Scaffolding Student Learning: Instructional Approaches and Issues*, New York, NY: University of Albany, State University of New York.

Laurillard, D. (2002), 'Rethinking Teaching for the Knowledge Society', *EDUCAUSE Review*, 37(1).

Lave, J. and E. Wenger (1991), *Situated Learning: Legitimate peripheral participation*, Cambridge: Cambridge University Press.

Novak, J. and M. Wurst (2003), *Supporting Communities of Practice through Personalization and Collaborative Structuring Based on Capturing Implicit Knowledge*, Proc. I-KNOW, Graz, 2003.

Salmon, G. (2004), *E-moderating: the key to teaching and learning online*, London: RoutledgeFalmer.

Smith, M.K. (2003), 'Communities of practice', the encyclopaedia of informal education. See www.infed.org/biblio/communities_of_practice.htm.

Stahl, G. (2005), *Group Cognition: Computer Support for Building Collaborative Knowledge*, MIT Press (in press, pub. 2006). Retrieved from http://www.cis.drexel.edu/faculty/gerry/mit/

Tennant, M. (1997), *Psychology and Adult Learning*, London: Routledge.

Urquhart, C., A. Yeoman and S. Sharp (2002), *NelH communities of practice evaluation report*, Aberystwyth: Department of Information and Library Studies, UWA. See http://www.nelh.nhs.uk.

Wenger, E. (1998), *Communities of Practice: Learning, meaning and identity*, Cambridge: Cambridge University Press.

14

e-Portfolios: A personal space for learning and the learner voice

Shane Sutherland

For e-portfolios to achieve their potential it is essential that they are not restricted by the demands of a single module, course or programme.

To state that e-portfolios provide a personal space for learning demands at least two qualifications: what is meant by an e-portfolio and what kinds of personal learning take place in this space?

e-Portfolios have burst upon us in double quick time: so speedily that any widely accepted definitions of what they are, what they do and who they are for still elude us. In this paper the e-portfolios described are the kind that belong to the learner not the institution; they are populated by the learner not their examiner; they are primarily concerned with supporting learning not assessment; they are for lifelong and life-wide learning not a single episode or a single course; they allow learners to present multiple stories of learning rather than being a simple aggregation of competencies; and, importantly, access to them is controlled by the learner who is able to invite feedback to support personal growth and understanding.

Tension resides in each of the dichotomies described above. When institutions provide e-portfolio systems for their constituents, they will probably expect a return on their investment, and the most obvious contender is the facility to capture learner data. However, an e-portfolio which supports a personal process of learning and which accommodates the recording of experience independent of place, time or context is not readily amenable to tracking or data harvesting. Institutions may want systems that measure how much of this skill, that experience or that knowledge is held within its community. For such information to be harvested the inputs must be described in a form which is understandable to the system which invariably means pre-populating the system with defined items: this cannot but depersonalize the process. The only way to develop an e-portfolio system capable of accommodating all of the things a learner experiences, learns or is able to do across their lived identities is to make the system very open and flexible. This, however, places the learner in control of describing who they are, what they know and what they can do, and this is unfamiliar territory for learner and institution alike.

If the learner is at the heart of the learning process, they must have absolute control of what is written, stored and shared in their e-portfolio. Knowing whether or not something s/he writes will be read by a particular audience will affect the voice of the author. Learners reflect more honestly, more openly and more willingly when they know that they control their own assets (items of value stored within an e-portfolio repository). Necessarily, certain items that are added to the e-portfolio are added as part of a controlled regime, for example, assessment or development planning. This requirement need not undermine the sense of the e-portfolio as a personal learning space because it is broadcast in advance that these assets are requisite for this purpose and so need to be shared with appropriate agents. The author's voice may be heard differently through these assets but that is known and to be expected. What is important is that the learner permits entry to view just those assets without compromising any of the larger collection of assets stored for other reasons.

It is the safety and security of the e-portfolio which makes it a place where learners 'reflect much more deeply than in paper-based alternatives' and where they can 'write and share things that [they] could never share in any other way'[1]. This sense of safe personal space would certainly be eroded if linked to any form of data-harvesting service, even if that service were ostensibly provided for the benefit of the learner.

We are defined by our stories of knowing, doing, sharing and relating: we are our stories. e-Portfolios, of the kind conceived here, allow learners to relate multiple stories to multiple audiences. Undoubtedly some of these stories will be structured, formal stories of knowing and understanding; designed for an audience responsible for evaluating the story against particular criteria. That an e-portfolio system can serve the institutional need for authentic assessment while still allowing learners to create their own stories of growth, of volunteering, of learning through hobbies and pastimes, and of values, interests and passions, is a bonus rather than a compromise. Institutional processes need not undermine the privacy of the e-portfolio; learner agency determines that even required stories are shared with others through choice, much like an essay formed on a personal computer only becomes public when it is handed-in.

Myriad learners have occupied the social learning spaces provided by chat tools like MSN and Habbo Hotel. There has been an explosion of WIKIs, WebLogs and social systems like Friendster, all of which have developed rapidly because they allow users to communicate with people they choose; on their terms; when they like. This really is personalized learning: learning made personal through choices enacted by the learner. A brief trawl of these spaces on the web will indicate that personalization is experienced less through customization of design and more through the ease with which learners can have their voice and their stories heard. It is this that has undoubtedly driven growth.

Early occupation of e-portfolio spaces will probably be driven by formal, or at least structured, initiatives within institutions: personal development planning (PDP) is the most apparent candidate. PDP is an attempt to encourage learners to reflect on their own progress, to plan development and to manage growth. In some respects it represents a move toward personalizing learning, and the e-portfolio provides the perfect system in which to plan for, chart and celebrate personal learning. PDP will be an institutional requirement but it is meant to be deeply personal; at its best it is concerned with making sense – of self, of subject and of community. This is personal learning, learning which is enhanced through critical self-reflection. e-Portfolios can be designed to encourage reflection, to prompt enquiry into why records or files are being stored, to provide opportunities for review over time and through providing tools which allow e-portfolio assets to be shared with others to promote social learning, feedback and support.

---

1   Reflective quotes are taken from a teacher and her student involved in a pilot e-portfolio project at the University of Wolverhampton.

For e-portfolios to achieve their potential it is essential that they are not restricted by the demands of a single module, course or programme. Each of us has many learning identities: as student; as worker; as hobbyist; as participant in life. e-Portfolios can provide the freedom for learners to capture pieces of their multi-faceted, complex and highly individual experiences and to weave those pieces into rich stories of learning: essentially they offer an exciting escape route from e-learning to me-learning.

Learning is life-wide and lifelong, though it is often characterized by episodes of learning; and while many episodes will be sequential, others will be concurrent. e-Portfolios designed for episodic learning tend to concentrate on recording the evidence required to prove knowledge, skills or ability relative to a particular course or programme. Once the requisite amount of evidence is collected, the e-portfolio is submitted for assessment, graded and archived. The evidence, having served its purpose, is rendered redundant. This application of e-portfolios misses entirely the complexity, connectedness and creativity of learning; it fails to value non-formal learning and precludes the joining up of that which has come before, alongside or after the episode. e-Portfolios as personal learning spaces allow learners to make connections between all aspects of their learning.

Linking e-portfolios to information systems can provide controlled and authoritative evidence of learning to support a learner's story. e-Portfolios for episodic learning should be thought of as learning (or learner) information systems rather than true e-portfolios. Their purpose is normally to track student behaviour as observed by an assessor or other agent, to record that behaviour against expected outcomes and to signal completion when all appropriate behaviours have been observed, assessed and validated. The record of this learning and the qualification to which it pertains can be presented as a digital synopsis and made available to the learner to use as evidence through the broader stories they tell in their e-portfolio for life.

So, to return to the beginning: e-portfolios for personal and personalized learning are the kind that belong to the learner not the institution; they are populated by the learner not their examiner; they are primarily concerned with supporting learning not assessment; they are for lifelong and life-wide learning not a single episode or a single course; they allow learners to present multiple stories of learning rather than being a simple aggregation of competencies; and, importantly, access to them is controlled by the learner who is able to invite feedback to support personal growth and understanding.

15

Designing Spaces for Personalizing Learning: Spaces for personalizing learning or personalizing spaces for learning?

Tom Franklin and Jill Armstrong

W e suggest … the need for a focus on spaces in which to personalize learning rather than on personalizing of spaces for learning.

Introduction

This paper argues that there are two potential purposes for personalizing learning spaces, and that they have different implications for the both the student's learning and the technology. The purposes can be understood as a space in which to personalize learning or personalizing of a space for learning. Note that the former is primarily pedagogic and the latter technical. If personalized learning is conceived as a problem of creating owned personalized space for learning, then customization of that space through the learner making choices leads to lack of potential interoperability and learning collaboration and a lack of maintaining or integrating any system over time. If personalized learning is conceived as a problem of creating owned personalized learning goals, then the system can be built around the pedagogic needs and does not need to lead to loss of interoperability or potential collaboration. Any customization here is at the margins because the choice and personalization is in the learning goals not the learning space. We outline a conceptual approach to both forms of personalizing, comment on learner motivation and then give focus to some issues involved in designing spaces for personalizing learning.

Conceptualizing personalized learning/personalization

'Personalizing learning' carries a range of potential meanings that are used in a variety of contexts, mostly without explanation. One way of grasping the conceptual thinking is to consider whether the idea of personalizing is being focused through the technology/space or whether the focus is through the learning. Secondly, to aid understanding, it is usually possible to consider the concept as a dichotomy, by providing it with a context. The following have been used to conceive the idea of personalizing learning.

Dichotomies

Focus of 'personalizing' on the space (system)

- Individualism/collaboration

- Customization/standardization

- Student designed or managed/institution designed or managed

- Personal space/classroom space

- De-institutionalized learner/institutionalized learner

- Individuated/community based

Focus of 'personalizing' on the learning

- *Pedagogy* led/systems led

- Reflection/transcript

- Learner centred/curriculum centred

- Learner centred/teacher centred

- Learner goals/formal education goals

- Personal ownership/institution ownership

These dichotomies provide conceptualizations that help us towards what needs to be considered in designing spaces for personalizing learning.

Design considerations

One of the keys to successfully building personalizable learning spaces is to understand the learner's motivation for wanting to customize their 'space' and have pedagogic and other tools needed to achieve their personal learning goals. Both appearance and function of a 'learning space' can be customised within the limits imposed by the need to maintain interoperability. Some motivations are:

- personal satisfaction

- to achieve a greater sense of ownership

- to embed the learning in other areas (notably work)

- to use preferred tools

- to build on previous work

- to use different devices (e.g. PCs, PDAs and Smartphones).

Tools need to be integrated so that meaningful workflows are supported. It is also essential that the ability to personalize does not drive systems to only offer the highest common factor in terms of functionality.

Designing effective 'spaces' for personalized learner goals, which allow for both customization and interoperability across the institution and beyond, presents considerable challenges in terms of design for learning. These include:

Learning

- **Support for negotiation with tutors, peers and employers.** This effectively means agreeing the learning goals, identifying the gap between them and the student's current understanding and, hence, the learning that is needed.

- **Support for integration of learning.** Lifelong learning means that learning is building on previous experience (education, work and leisure). At the very least, the student should be able to integrate all their learning from disparate sources into a meaningful whole that includes more than simply linking units of learning together. An interesting model here might be 'TheBrain' (www.thebrain.com).

- **Support for integration of learning with work and leisure.** This assumes that learning has some goal – whether instrumental or personal development – and means that the learning space needs very strong links into other spaces, which implies the need for common standards and ways of linking the learning into those other spaces and information, discussions and activities in those spaces into the learning space.

Teaching and course development

Many of the issues for teaching are the same as for learning; however, there are also a number of considerations around design to support personal learning, so as well as the ones discussed above there is:

- support for development of courses including locating and assembling content

- support for diagnostics and personal course planning

- support for content re-use.

Customization

Customization can occur at the student, course or institutional level. Should the student (or teacher) be able to make the learning space look and behave differently on different courses? There will be tensions between the customizations that the teacher produces for effective teaching and personalizations that the student wants for effective learning, and this may be critical to the entire enterprise of personalization.

Customization is required at the student level, particularly if we are to meet the DfES strategy, which wants to, 'Provide a personalized online learning space for every learner,' and that 'in the future it will be ... a digital space that is personalized, that remembers what the learner is interested in and suggests relevant web sites, or alerts them to courses and learning opportunities that fit their needs' (DfES, 2005). Here we are moving beyond simple customization/personalization to a much more active role for the learning space that encompasses push technologies based on a complex model of the student's current knowledge, motivations and goals, but raises questions of who controls this (the individual, the institution or the state).

Finally, customization occurs at a number of different levels within the learning space:

- the appearance (or skin)
- the tools available
- the way the tools behave.

Interoperability

To enable students to have personalizable and customizable learning spaces interoperability will be required between systems – both technical systems and institutional systems (schools/colleges/universities/employment). Currently these are still in their infancy, with standards primarily concerned with the syntax used to exchange information. Without a rich shared semantic model, however, it will be difficult to exchange data between systems. Thus we will need:

- technical standards for interoperability that work across institutions and technologies and time
- system level structures that support sharing of information (cross-institutional integration).

Learning spaces – as metaphors

'Learning space' is only one of many ways of conceptualizing the presentation to the learner of their learning, and a number of specific 'space' metaphors could be selected that help the learner in understanding the purpose and potential of the 'space'. Each metaphor opens up many ideas on how to engage with the environment, but equally closes down others.

Classroom

Many virtual learning environments have elements that relate to classrooms and classroom management – with the lecturer having control and issuing content as it is needed. This is unsurprising as it is usual for new technologies to mimic the old before expanding to undertake previously impossible activities.

Desk

This is a particular type of space and is the one that is familiar both from the real world and from the virtual world (where it is the metaphor used by Windows). It suggests a particular method of working and of organizing one's information.

Communication centre

A completely different way of thinking about virtual environments is to consider them as communication centres which provide access to a wide variety of different channels and resources (people, documents, and so on). The model requires re-thinking the way that we design interfaces and use the computer, but relates more closely to some of the pedagogic models that focus on communication, collaboration and engagement rather than content.

Personal organizer

Personal Digital Organizers (or PDAs) loosely follow a metaphor of the personal organizer with sections for diaries, address books, to-do lists, notes, and so on, with other functionality coming later. Consequently they have a very different look and feel to the desktop PC or laptop, and this is not just because of the different form factor and lack of a keyboard.

Portfolio

An interesting metaphor might be the learning environment as portfolio. This would then build on other important strategies from the DfES, HEFCE, and so on, on the use of portfolios, and would put at the centre of the learning space the collection of evidence of learning and reflection upon learning.

Study with meeting room

A study would clearly indicate that it is a space owned by the learner, to be organized to their needs. This creates a clear recognition about ownership and purpose and if each study has an adjoining 'meeting room' where collaboration and communications can be pursued, both individual and collaborative needs can be met.

In short then, the metaphor that underlies systems has an extremely powerful impact on what the users can do most readily and how we engage with them. Whether users will be able to choose systems that reflect their preferred metaphor will have a huge impact.

Conclusion

We have argued for clarity in both the discourse on personalizing learning and how we conceive this to ensure a common understanding and approach to thinking and development of personalization. For effective design of learning spaces we suggest the need for an appropriate metaphor for 'personalized learning spaces' and we have considered the need for a focus on spaces in which to personalize learning rather than on personalizing of spaces for learning. Forms of customization can support this aim, but customization needs to operate within systems that are interoperable and can be integrated and sustained over time.

References

DfES (2005), *e-Strategy: Harnessing Technology*, Nottingham: DfES Publications.

16

Personalized Learning and Accessibility: Adaptability at the point of delivery

Alistair McNaught and John Sewell

I n a learning context, it is important to recognize that the accessibility of the learning experience may be more significant than the accessibility of the resource.

The role of personalization in meeting learner needs

Debates about personalization cover a wide field from learning theory to instructional design. In the arguments below we focus on the ability of the learner to adapt the resources with which they interact in a learning experience. Traditional teaching resources – books, overhead transparencies, videos and handouts – are very limited in the personalization available because they lack adaptability. By contrast, learners using ICT to access materials or produce responses have a medium that allows many individual needs to be satisfied by personalizing the interface. Adaptations may range from using a trackball to changing the font style, size or colour, or having text spoken out.

The changes that are appropriate for an individual will differ with circumstances and time. For example, the interface may be arranged and driven differently when working on a train to working in a classroom or an office. It may be different again if the learner has a sprained wrist or other injury. Where difficulties in using the conventional interface are more permanent (e.g. an impairment or disability) then the benefits of adapting the interface are disproportionately large. Without adaptation the user may be unable to access the materials at all. The number of learners in this position is not small and is constantly changing. Forrester research for Microsoft (Microsoft, 2004) indicates that 60 per cent of working age Americans are likely or very likely to need the accessibility features built in to the Windows operating system. The ability to adapt a resource or an interface brings benefits to many, but for those with a disability its effects are disproportionately valuable, making access possible where otherwise it would be impossible.

The responsibility for personalization

Across the spectrum of personalization the learner will always have the prime responsibility in deciding what is appropriate from the options available. The learner will usually have executive responsibility where the issues are simple, but even where they are complex, and specialists and special equipment and software are involved, it is still the responsibility of the learner to make the primary decision. Unfortunately the learner rarely has the knowledge to know the range of solutions available. Within many institutions it is not uncommon for staff to be equally untrained as to the range of approaches available. Discussion threads on the FE 'ILT champions' mailing list have highlighted difficulties in some colleges where the Information Learning Technology (ILT) champions have good knowledge of software capability but little awareness of the accessibility needs the software might meet. Meanwhile, colleagues supporting disabled learners in HE and FE may have more experience with particular disabilities than with rapidly advancing technologies.

In a learning environment, many people influence the ease with which personalization and adaptation take place. It is not just an issue for professional materials developers meeting accessibility standards. Many materials a learner encounters are produced locally by lecturers and practitioners, and it is the responsibility of those involved in the delivery and use of those materials to ensure that when the materials are needed by the learner they can be accessed. Learners may access and use materials in many ways, under many circumstances and at different times. The responsibility for supporting personalization and adaptability therefore lies with teaching staff and developers, learning resource staff, IT support, learner support, staff developers and managers. There are training implications across the different roles in an institution, not least because many potential solutions already exist but are unrecognized by either staff or students.

Alternative fixes for accessibility problems

In a learning context, it is important to recognize that the accessibility of the learning experience may be more significant than the accessibility of the resource. For example, an e-resource may be inherently adaptable – with customizable fonts, colours and user control of animations, and so on – but if it is delivered in a lecture context, the accessibility options will be lost to the disabled user.

Conversely, a resource with low adaptability could form part of an accessible learning experience in one of two ways. The teaching can be adapted; for example, a photocopied handwritten resource (with inherently poor accessibility) can have the key points read out to stimulate a discussion. Alternatively, a magnifying sheet might be used by a visually impaired learner.

It is thus possible to identify three ways of potentially fixing an inaccessible learning experience: a hardware fix, a software fix or a pedagogical fix.

- A **hardware fix** might include a range of options from magnifying sheets to colour filters, joysticks, tracker balls or switch input. The hardware fix provides a personalized solution via personalized kit.

- **Software fixes** might include specific applications (e.g. screen magnifiers, screen readers, text to speech, and so on) or generic options (altering font size, style and colour on a browser). Any software fix provides potential challenges; for example, training, networking and licence management. But more significantly, software fixes also provide potential quick wins. Learners who become confident at exploiting the accessibility features of software have a transferable skill that encourages independence in a wider range of contexts – one of the ultimate goals of teaching.

- **Pedagogical fixes** are tutor/lecturer dependent and will depend on the skills, training, experience and creativity of the tutor/lecturer. In many contexts these fixes can be very effective. They have the advantages of being sustainable, adaptable and self-reinforcing. Realistically, however, the range of pedagogical approaches open to teaching staff can be constrained by factors as diverse as class size, room layout, availability of ICT infrastructure and – critically – effective staff development. The accessibility of a learning experience, therefore, does not lend itself to a set of checklists but rather a set of values, opportunities and responsibilities.

Issues around effective design

Describing a learning resource as accessible or inaccessible is unhelpful. Most resources are highly accessible to some learners in some contexts. None are accessible to all learners in all contexts. A key issue often overlooked in the accessibility/personalization debate is the subject of context sensitivity. There are excellent guidelines for expert e-content providers creating materials for mass audiences with unknown accessibility needs. Some organizations (e.g. the National Learning Network, 2005) provide their own detailed interpretations of the guidelines for e-content producers. Good though they are, such guidelines are inadequate for creating a culture of adaptable, personalizable resources.

A successful learning institution is characterized by many qualities, one of which is the ability of teachers/lecturers to create their own teaching materials adapted to the needs, interests and aspirations of the learners. In most quality institutions a significant proportion of the resources in use are original creations or adaptations produced by the teacher/lecturer. For these people, technical guidelines for the accessibility of online resources may be meaningless. In fact they may be counterproductive by raising barriers to the creation of e-learning materials, forcing a retreat to 'safer' traditional methods (using books and handouts is rarely criticized). Ironically, e-resources are inherently MORE accessible than traditional resources yet accessibility advisors are quicker to ban 'inaccessible' e-resources from the network than they are to ban books, videos or audio tapes from the library.

To develop an effective approach to adaptable e-learning, institutions need to take a holistic, learning-centred view of accessibility. This may involve strategically and pragmatically ignoring recommended practice. For example, it is normally desirable to provide alternative text descriptions (ALT tags) for significant images on a web page but it may not be appropriate if:

- The text description undermines the learning objectives of an online assessment by giving the answer away.

- The described image is a poorer resource than an alternative learning experience – a description of a satellite image would be a poor substitute for a tactile version, yet the former (by meeting accessibility checklists) might discourage the latter.

- The ALT tag description is an excuse for a poorer text narrative (e.g. 'Glasgow from the air').

Creating a culture of adaptability

This paper has focused on a relatively narrow area of personalization – the ability of the user to adapt a resource or a learning experience to suit their accessibility needs. For this modest goal to be achieved we have identified a need for institution-wide awareness raising so that the different roles within the organization recognize their mutual dependencies in supporting accessibility at the point of delivery. As soon as different players in the institution start to take their responsibilities seriously contradictions will arise – the policy for network security may clash with the policy for accessibility, for example. Dialogues will need to take place and compromises will need to be reached. There are implications for staff training, student training, communication structures, decision making and documentation mechanisms. The learners – with and without accessibility needs – should be involved appropriately, not least because many issues will have no right solution so at least should have a democratic one where the stakeholders are involved.

The JISC TechDis service (www.techdis.ac.uk) has developed a range of support materials, including role-based guidance for education institutions in the post-16 sector. But personalization of learning is still at an immature stage of development. The issues – as argued in other papers in this volume – go beyond technology to philosophy, learning theory and politics. Advice will necessarily change as practice develops. Nevertheless, the TechDis website offers free downloadable staff training packs. Sample resources in the 'Creation of learning materials' section illustrate how resources can be made accessible to a wider range of learners using the functionality built into common office applications (e.g. styles, hyperlinks, screen tips, inserting audio, and so on). None of these resources or techniques will meet all accessibility needs, but building staff skills is an iterative process. Individuals have unique training needs and preferences. Personalized learning applies to the way we educate staff as well as students.

Conclusion

The personalization agenda is particularly pertinent for disabled learners; resources that are adaptable at the point of delivery may give disproportionate benefits to students with accessibility needs. Accessibility may be related to the nature of the resource and the hardware/software available, but the pedagogical approach can be of overriding significance. Advice on the creation of adaptable e-resources needs to be carefully targeted to the skills, influences and responsibility of the staff concerned. Embedding a culture of adaptable personalized learning will involve institution-wide communication, collaboration and compromise – processes in which the learners should have a defined and respected role. Increasing staff skills and confidence in e-learning improves their ability to create adaptable resources and adaptable learning experiences.

References

Microsoft (2004), 'The Wide Range of Abilities and Its Impact on Computer Technology'. See www.microsoft.com/enable/research/default.aspx.

National Learning Network advice for e-content creators (2005), www. nln.ac.uk/materials/developers/technical_accessibility_requirements.asp?menuitem=technical& pid).

17

Personalized e-Learning in Primary and Secondary Education: The impact of inconsistent definitions and goals

Rachada Monthienvichienchai

The most personalized learning experience ... [is one where] the student and the teacher are reflecting on and reacting to the individual experience of the student.

Introduction

The current emphasis of personalized e-learning has so far been placed on providing adaptive content to match a certain profile of the learner, and the contentious point of debate is on what elements of such a profile should an adaptive virtual learning environment (VLE) adapt to and how. For example, the EU-funded 3DE project (www.3deproject.com) takes on the challenge of personalizing e-learning by matching learning content to a learner's learning style profile (in 3DE's case, the Kolb learning style model), while other projects, such as ActiveMath (Melis and Andrès, 2005) and APeLS (Conlan and Wade, 2004), adapt to the learner's prior knowledge and learning goals. From such projects, critics and advocates for particular adaptation parameters have emerged with equal numbers of arguments for and against personalizing to each parameter, with some even questioning the effectiveness of personalizing learning in the first place (Marzano, 1998).

However, this paper argues that conclusions cannot be drawn concerning the effectiveness or appropriateness of personalizing learning and the parameters for adaptation without first formalizing what exactly is the definition and therefore the goals of personalization in e-learning. Any conclusions concerning effectiveness of personalization must be made with respect to and within the context of such a definition. For example, critics of VLEs that provide the learner with contents that only match his or her learning style profile have a valid argument in that such strategy will not create a better learner, but one with the ability to learn only from limited types of learning material (Coffield et al., 2004). However, if a VLE's goal for personalizing is to act only as a supporting learning tool to compliment and enhance other learning resources and activities, then the ability to provide the student with materials that match a particular learning preference or style becomes an added-value feature of the VLE. On the other hand, if the same VLE aims to act in the role of a personal tutor, then such a strategy would be wholly inadequate for the task, as not only will the student be getting a limited subset of learning material, but he or she will also be deprived of learning tasks that will develop him or her as a lifelong learner.

Goals of personalized e-learning

From the limited examples given above, it is apparent that the goals of personalization play an important role in determining not only what will be considered as effective personalization, but also what the personalization strategy should be, that is, what is 'personalization'.

In order to concretize this argument, the goals of personalizing e-learning in the primary and secondary education sectors that have been adopted by an EU-funded project – iClass (www.iclass.info) – are presented below. Each of these goals is then placed within the context of a three-tier personalization framework. The aim is to explicitly show how the reason behind personalization at each tier affects the strategy for personalization and therefore how its effectiveness can be evaluated – underlining the importance of establishing the goals of personalization.

'Class' goals for personalization

As mentioned above, the first step for effective personalized e-learning is to define what the VLE hopes to achieve through personalization – without clear goals, effective decisions concerning personalization strategies cannot be made. In iClass, personalization aims to:

- Minimize the number of irrelevant or inappropriate learning contents and activities that the student will be presented with when interacting with iClass.

- Create a 'polyvalent' learner who has the learning skills to learn with many different types of learning contents and learning activities. This is especially important in the primary and secondary education sector.

- Provide mentoring guidance to the learner when required – that is, take on the role of a personal tutor.

Personalized support for communal curriculum

An important distinction that has been made in defining the goals of personalization in iClass is the difference between a personalized curriculum and personalized support for students completing an un-personalized or communal curriculum (e.g. GCSE Mathematics). In the former case (personalized curriculum), personalization strategies need to consider not only how the student will be taught, but also what the student will be learning in the first place. In the latter case, the curriculum has already been set and the main aim of the personalization strategies is to provide effective support for the student to complete such a curriculum. iClass personalization strategies are consistent with the latter case in that they aim to provide personalized support for multiple communal curricula set by each education ministry in the European Union. The pretext for choosing this approach to personalization (as opposed to providing a personalized curriculum) is the need to preserve the value of education within society while also meeting the different needs of individual students who will positively contribute to society. The project believes that an individualistic approach to education, at least in the primary and secondary school sector, will result in students with understanding of the domain that does not align with relevant communities of practice and personal value that is detached from society.

Three-tier personalization framework

To meet the personalization goals of iClass, the project has adopted the following high-level three-tier personalization framework (a draft version of which was first presented in Melis and Monthienvichienchai, 2004) for formalizing its strategies for personalizing teaching and learning activities in its VLE. The three tiers are:

- customization
- contextualization
- individualization.

At the *customization* tier, the aim is to provide a learning environment that is compatible with the technical infrastructure that is available for the teacher and/or the student. For example, do students have access to ubiquitous computing devices and do they have access to pen-based input devices? At this level, personalization aims to eliminate learning activities that are impossible for students to take part in owing to technical limitations of the students' (school's or teacher's) e-learning environment. The result of this is a subset of learning activities from all activities that are available in the VLE.

At the *contextualization* tier, the VLE aims to identify within the subset of learning activities that resulted from customization another subset of learning activities that would be appropriate for the student, given his/her learning context. The parameters that have been identified for adaptation at this tier include:

- language of the learning material
- curriculum
- syllabus
- topic
- learning goals
- prior knowledge of the student.

Again, the result of applying this tier of personalization is another subset of learning activities. At both of these tiers, the effectiveness of the personalization process can be assessed by how well the VLE has managed to match the learning activities provided with each of the parameters in the profile of the learner. The optimum result, therefore, is that the subset of learning activities consists of only activities that match these parameters. So far, the personalization process has succeeded in achieving only the first of three iClass goals for personalization – minimizing irrelevant learning activities.

However, at the third tier – *individualization* – the two other goals of iClass (creating a polyvalent learner and provision of mentoring guidance) demand a significant change in the personalization strategy. The focus and goal of personalization is no longer eliminating irrelevance, but enabling the student to effectively consume and navigate through the learning activities that remain – a challenge that is being partially met through techniques such as adaptive navigational support (Brusilovsky *et al.*, 1996). Within this subset of learning activities, the student has the potential to develop as a learner unhindered by irrelevant inappropriate activities, while under the guidance of the VLE.

Personalization and individualization

The main challenge at this tier, therefore, is one of how to provide the right guidance and support for the student. This, in fact, is where the learning (and teaching) will happen. iClass tackles the personalization challenge at this level in several ways:

- **Encapsulation of 'best' teaching/learning practice**: iClass uses and makes available to the student and teacher multiple teaching and learning strategies that have proven to be effective in the domain that the student is in. This gives both the teacher and the student the ability to learn one topic from several different teaching/learning strategies. Note that at this stage it is not the relevance of learning activities that is the main concern of personalization, but how those activities are presented to the student: the linear and non-linear narratives.

- **Support student's metacognitive reflection of his/her learning experience** to empower both the student and the teacher to improve the learning experience. This is the most personalized learning experience, as the student and the teacher are reflecting on and reacting to the individual experience of the student. iClass aims to implement effective tracking and presentation of the learner's learning history to enable students and teacher to determine whether there are learning patterns that can be improved on, for example the learner is tackling the topic in too shallow a manner or that the learner has not interacted with enough content or activities within a particular topic. The tracking data, if shared among other students, can also allow the student to learn from another student's experience, thus supporting the creation of a community of learners through personalized learning reflection.

- **Provision of learning support tools**, such as mind-mapping and rich media editing tool, to enable students to learn effectively with different types of learning material even if the material does not match the preferred style of learning of the student. This aims to help create the polyvalent learner.

The final tier of the personalization framework presents the most challenge for personalization in VLEs as it represents a transition from what computers can do best (precisely matching search results with certain search criteria) to what humans can do best (providing rich contextual adaptive guidance to the learner). However, what is important to underline is that the definition of 'personalization' is very different at each tier and for each goal. Consequently, the strategies and evaluation criteria for personalization in e-learning need to reflect this difference.

Conclusions

This paper has critically examined what the term 'personalization' means in the e-learning context. It has argued that 'personalization', in the context of e-learning, is too broad and generic for a specific personalization strategy to be derived for implementation in VLEs. Personalization strategies need to be as different and diverse as the students that they are trying to support. No single definition of personalization will be valid for all use cases and contexts. Any implementation and evaluation of personalization must be made with respect to the definitions, goals and contexts of personalization.

In order to concretize the above argument, a three-tier personalization framework adopted by the iClass project has been presented, differentiating between multiple personalization strategies that need to be implemented in order to achieve effective learner-centred e-learning. What is clear from this formalization of the personalization process is that providing the appropriate learning content and activities is only a partial implementation of personalized e-learning. Effective personalization will need to take into account the need to produce better – polyvalent – learners in all environments, not just an adaptive one. When personalizing learning – especially for use in the primary and secondary school sector – learning skills need to be developed together with domain knowledge. Lastly, personalized e-learning in today's environment would also need to take into account the everyday practice in today's teaching and learning environments, e.g. classroom setup, teacher's workflow and workload. Some outstanding questions concerning the human factors of personalized e-learning include:

- What is the best practice for teaching a class in which students' computer-based activities are personalized?

- What teaching support tools will be required when teaching with personalized activities (organizational as well as classroom teaching material)?

- How can we maintain relevance of personalized learning with respect to communities of practice?

- What are the limits for personalizing learning? Some countries provide a curriculum that allows for more personalized approaches to learning than others.

As well as ensuring that personalization is carried out effectively, adequate considerations for these issues must also be taken to ensure that personalized e-learning will gain mass-adoption in the primary and secondary education sector. Without such consideration, personalized learning will have significant difficulties in gaining grass-root support with or without the drive from central government.

Acknowledgements

This paper is partly a result of research conducted within the iClass project, funded under the 6th Framework Programme of the European Community (IST 507922). The author is solely responsible for its content. The European Community is not responsible for any use that might be made of information appearing herein.

References

Brusilovsky, P., E. Schwarz and G. Weber (1996), 'A tool for developing hypermedia-based ITS on WWW', paper presented at the Proceedings of Workshop 'Architectures and Methods for designing Cost-Effective and Reusable ITSs' at the Third International Conference on Intelligent Tutoring Systems, ITS-96, Montreal.

Coffield, F., K. Ecclestone, E. Hall and D. Moseley (2004), *Learning Styles and Pedagogy in Post 16 Education*, London: Learning and Skills Development Agency. See www.ncl.ac.uk/ecls/research/education/cll/research/LearnStylesPedPost16.htm.

Conlan, O. and V. Wade (2004), 'Evaluation of APeLS: An Adaptive eLearning Service based on the Multi-model, Metadata-driven Approach', paper presented at Third International Conference on Adaptive Hypermedia and Adaptive Web-Based Systems (AH2004) Proceedings, Eindhoven, The Netherlands.

Marzano, R.J. (1998), *A theory-based meta-analysis of research on instruction*, Aurora, CO: Mid-continent Regional Educational Laboratory.

Melis, E. and E. Andrès (2005), 'Global Feedback in ActiveMath', in *International Journal of Computers in Mathematics and Science Teaching*, 24(2), AACE, pp. 197–220.

Melis, E. and R. Monthienvichienchai (2004), 'They Call It Learning Style But It's So Much More', *World Conference on E-Learning in Corporate, Government, Health, & Higher Education*, 2004(1), Washington, DC: E-Learning, pp. 1383–1390.

18

Personal Learning with Mobile and Wireless Technologies

Ros Smith

From the pedagogical point of view, connectivity on location enables more emphasis on discovery-based, problem-solving and collaborative learning.

This paper is based on the illustrations and related discussion of practice with mobile and wireless technologies which can be found in a recent publication, 'Innovative Practice with e-Learning', JISC (2005), from the Innovation strand of the JISC e-Learning Programme (www.jisc.ac.uk/elearning).

The practice illustrated in this cross-sector publication indicates that a number of important benefits are possible for learners who are able to make use of mobile devices. These have been identified as:

- portability

- any time, anywhere connectivity

- flexible and timely access to e-learning resources

- immediacy of communication

- empowerment and engagement of learners, particularly those in dispersed communities

- active learning experiences.

In particular, there is much valuable evidence in the ten case studies of the potential of mobile and wireless technologies to support individualized learning. Although it must be stressed that most institutions and practitioners are a long way from embedding mobile and wireless learning in standard everyday practice, the case studies illustrate ways in which this could happen, or is already happening, in the work of innovative practitioners. There are clearly challenges to overcome, including evidence from one case study from Sussex University[1] that students can be reluctant to use the more complex mobile devices in a learning context, perhaps because of their association with leisure and lifestyle, or simply because they had already made their own choice of third-generation mobile phone and did not wish to use another.

Despite this, 'Innovative Practice with e-Learning' shows that mobile and wireless technologies can offer particular benefits in supporting learners' personal routes to conceptual understanding or skills acquisition. This is especially the case where mobile devices can link

---

1   A digital key to productive learning, University of Sussex, JISC, (2005). See www.jisc.ac.uk/eli_casestudies.html.

to a wireless network or to the internet. Evidence has been drawn from adult and community learning and further and higher education institutions. Details of each of the following case studies can be found on JISC's website (www.jisc.ac.uk/eli_casestudies.html).[2]

Taking technology to the learner – Gloucestershire College of Arts and Technology

As part of the lifelong learning strategy at the college, an outreach service has brought ICT classes to adult learners unable to attend college classes. Further education colleges have offered ICT classes in community venues for some time, but difficulties with broadband connectivity have restricted the range and flexibility of provision.

The solution came in the form of a mobile laptop scheme run in conjunction with a satellite communication van. This initiative has given basic ICT skills tuition a community and personal focus. Projects generated by the learners themselves, for example the creation of a website for the local village, have tapped into learners' existing knowledge and interests. Achievements are measured in personal terms in the most part, although opportunities to progress on to assessed courses are available, if required.

> *I've still got schoolchildren and they're magic on the computers, so I thought, 'I'm not going to let them beat me'.* (Ron Bockhart, adult ICT learner)

Active, collaborative learning – University of Strathclyde

An electronic voting system, Interwrite™ PRS (Personal Response System), has been adopted in the Department of Mechanical Engineering to increase interactivity in lectures. Four large lecture rooms have been equipped with infra-red voting devices and receivers, and curved rows of seats added, to enable students to engage in group discussion in response to multiple choice questions designed by lecturers to establish conceptual knowledge. The results have shown an increase in student attendance and achievement as a result of these opportunities to test out and develop personal interpretations with other students.

> *It helps you to learn to stand up for yourself and argue your point of view… To be able to sit there and say that you are wrong is difficult for anybody, but in there it is easier because there are 50 per cent that were wrong as well.* (Student quote, Evaluation Data, Nicol and Boyle, 2003)

Mobile learning and teaching with PDAs – Dewsbury College, Thomas Danby College and Bishop Burton College

These FE colleges in Yorkshire have experimented with use of resources on Personal Digital Assistants (PDAs) to widen participation by disadvantaged groups, and to provide access to e-learning resources in outreach and work-based environments.

---

2   Interviews for the case studies were conducted by a team from the Open University led by Dr Agnes Kukulska-Hulme. See www.jisc.ac.uk/eli_oucasestudies.html.

Dewsbury College staff have used web pages scaled down to fit the smaller screen of the PDA, with hyperlinks to video and audio files, to help learners on National Vocational Qualifications (NVQ) child care courses in outreach venues gain access to e-learning. At Thomas Danby College, resources in Macromedia® Flash® have been used by basic skills learners in 'drill for skill' activities in work-based learning. Both of these examples give evidence of how placing the technology literally in their hands has empowered learners by enabling them to control the pace of their learning and the sequence of resources they use. Where they own their own handheld device, or are able to acquire one on loan from the institution, learners are also able to control the place and time of their learning activities as well.

> *We have each got our own PDA which we use in groups or individually, and it's got links to the web pages. First the teacher uses them on the projector, using a laptop. We've got the same information, but we have got it in our hands, in our control.* (Child care NVQ Level 3 student, Sure Start Centre, Dewsbury)

Designing flexible learning spaces – Northumbria University

Designing activities that provide opportunities for personalizing the learning process, for example by choosing the place, time, medium and frequency in which learners or students access learning materials, is a challenge that practitioners now need to address. Evidence that this is understood by higher education institutions comes from this case study. This gives an account of how a university library service has re-evaluated the way its learning spaces are managed in response to changes in course demands and students' needs. Where an institution is able to offer a variety of learning spaces, some with informal seating and café facilities, and loan schemes for wireless laptops, learners have appreciated the increased flexibility.

> *Talk to and observe your learners. In a library, watch how students use resources, even down to where chairs are left at night. Build an evidence base against which to check your understanding and evaluate new developments by means of user surveys.* (Professor Jane Core, Director of Learning Resources, Northumbria University)

These examples indicate some of the benefits that use of mobile and wireless technologies offers for learners. They can extend the reach, and in some cases, add to the immediacy of e-learning and may deepen individuals' conceptual understanding through opportunities for dialogue and debate. However, they do not benefit all individuals in the same way. 'Innovative Practice with e-Learning' also covers the benefits and constraints of using mobile devices with disabled learners, where the picture is more ambiguous.

Mobile devices can offer some important advantages to learners with disabilities:

- participation in activities that might otherwise be inaccessible
- portable access to appropriately designed e-learning resources
- avoidance of some of the self-image problems associated with assistive technologies
- opportunities for self-paced use of learning resources in any context.

For many disabled learners, mobile phones really do add value, for example SMS messaging and email can help deaf learners work on collaborative tasks on an almost equal footing with their non-signing peers. The ability to beam files wirelessly between devices can also mean that collaborative tasks are made easier for many disabled learners. However, individuals' needs will differ markedly and the most clear-cut constraint is that of small screen and keyboard size for learners with visual or motor impairment.

On the other hand, benefits have also been recorded for institutional practice, for example in improving the efficiency of capture and management of learner data through wireless-enabled attendance registration. Data collected by staff with tablet PCs is then channelled into personalized home pages for learners on the institution's Managed Learning Environment.[3] Many institutions and organizations are also finding use of less sophisticated tools such as mobile phones and SMS messaging equally valuable in maintaining contact with learners in ways that can be made more relevant and personal to them. It could be argued that making learning more 'personal' is not just about supporting individual learners, but also about helping institutions to achieve their goals in relation to enabling successful and effective learning.

It is safest not to overestimate the potential of mobile and wireless technologies – learning and teaching are unlikely to be wholly transformed by their arrival. Evidence from these case studies suggests that mobile devices *can* increase learners' sense of control over their learning. Spontaneity of access to e-learning content and communication tools *can* enable individuals to decide when and where certain aspects of learning can take place and, with access to the internet, even to define the parameters of that learning for themselves. Institutions may also benefit in the long term, but this will, in turn, pose challenges in assuring the quality of learning that can be delivered via mobile as well as e-learning. Policies regarding access to the network from handheld devices owned by learners and practitioners and software and hardware that can be supported by the institution are further decisions that mobile and wireless access to e-learning will necessitate.

References

JISC (2005), *Innovative Practice with e-Learning*. See www.jisc.ac.uk/eli_practice.html.

Kukulska-Hulme, A., S. Heppell, A. Jeffs and A. Nicholson (2005), *Case Studies of Innovative Practice*. See www.jisc.ac.uik/eli_oucasestudies.html.

Nicol, D.J. and Boyle, J.T. (2003), 'Peer Instruction versus Class-wide Discussion in large classes: a comparison of two interaction methods in the wired classroom', *Studies in Higher Education*, 28(4), October.

---

3 Changing to a wireless world, Ealing, Hammersmith and West London College, JISC (2005). www.jisc.ac.uk/eli_casestudies.html.

19

Enabling Personalization through Context Awareness

Laura Naismith

The widespread use of mobile technologies also opens up new possibilities for promoting collaborative construction of context.

Introduction

In traditional computing, context is generally viewed as a conceptual 'shell' that surrounds an individual. In this model, a variety of sensors are used to gather information about the individual's physical environment, and this information is used to adapt the content or interface or make suggestions to the user as to what actions he or she may like to take next. User profile information may also be used, but usually in a static way. This model of context is essentially reactive; the system is continually responding to the user's current state in order to offer recommendations or take sensible actions.

We propose that context does not exist outside of an individual, but is rather a dynamic process of interaction between an individual and his or her physical and social environment, with historical dependencies. Context can be viewed as 'a set of changing relationships that may be shaped by the history of those relationships' (Lonsdale et al., 2003, p. 81). This model is inclusive of traditional context features such as time and location, but also pushes the envelope of context to include user characteristics, previous knowledge, interests and motivations and current trajectories through physical and virtual space. In addition to providing the reactive capabilities of the traditional model, we can also use context proactively to support future planning. This can include making choices between immediate alternatives, making predictions about the likely outcomes of various actions and personal development planning.

Personalized learning is about giving learners control over what, where, when and how they will learn. By identifying, using and representing appropriate contextual features, we can help users to interact with their environments in a highly personal way, thus promoting engaging and effective personalized learning.

Designing context aware systems

The socio-cognitive engineering methodology (Sharples et al., 2002) is our basis for the design of usable, useful and elegant systems that utilize contextual features appropriately and effectively to support individuals in their learning. In the initial activity analysis stage, a set of general system requirements is extended through both theoretical investigation and field studies of prospective learners to develop a task model. The task model helps to illuminate the important contextual features from the learner's physical and social environments and provides an insight into how context might be best represented back to the learner, such as through an open learner model (Bull and McEvoy, 2003). The activity analysis stage is followed by an iterative process of design and evaluation. As the deployment of complex human-centred technology may in itself affect ways of learning and interacting, the outcome of the methodology is rarely a single product, but rather 'a continuing process of analysis, design, implementation, deployment, further analysis and refinement' (Sharples *et al.*, 2002, p. 322).

The following projects represent ongoing work at the University of Birmingham to develop and implement our contextual model. These systems support learners both in reacting to their surroundings through *reflection-in-context* and proactively planning for future learning activities through *reflection-on-context*.

CAGE (Context Aware Gallery Explorer)

CAGE provides a mechanism for selecting, filtering and presenting relevant content to visitors in an art gallery via a handheld device. The system is based on the hierarchical model of context developed within the MOBIlearn project (Lonsdale *et al.*, 2003). In this model, a context state provides a current snapshot of the learner's context process. A context substate is the set of those elements from the context state that are directly relevant to the current learning focus. Context features are the individual elements found within a context substate, such as time, location and a learner's interests. Data relating to context features are gathered either automatically or through user input. The values of the context features can either be used to exclude irrelevant content or to rank content in terms of relevance.

In practice, CAGE is able to provide a rich experience for visitors using relatively few context features to derive a context substate (Lonsdale *et al.*, 2004). The current learning topic is indicated by the visitor, or obtained from his or her profile. An ultrasonic location tracking system is able to determine the visitor's absolute location within the gallery and calculate which exhibit he or she is closest to. Time spent at each exhibit is used as an indicator of interest in the exhibit itself, while the history of the visitor's previous interactions in the gallery space is used to determine interest in relationships between exhibits. Content is pushed to the visitor's handheld device based on these features, but the visitor is also supported in undertaking reflection-in-context to question the system's recommendations, and specify new learning topics and goals. CAGE's implementation of context awareness helps maintain the visitor's attention on the current situation, but also provides the ability for visitors to take advantage of serendipitous learning opportunities.

CAERUS (Context Aware Educational Resource System)

CAERUS (Naismith, Ting and Sharples, 2005) is designed to engage visitors to outdoor tourist locations and environmental centres through the use of location-aware mobile technology. A desktop authoring application is used to divide a site map up into physical regions. Each region can be associated with one or more themes. Themes represent a particular perspective on a multi-faceted artefact or exhibit and can be used to group media such as text, audio, video and web pages. The artefacts or exhibits that best represent a particular perspective then form the basis for a multimedia tour.

As they move around within the physical space, visitors using the CAERUS handheld application on a mobile device automatically receive audio content relevant to their physical location, as determined by a GPS sensor, and specific to their chosen theme. As with CAGE, this helps their attention to remain focused on the surrounding physical environment. A clear push-button interface on the handheld enables the visitor to control further navigation of provided content. Visitors can also retrace their paths through the outdoor site to revisit previously viewed content. In this way, CAERUS supports enhanced situated learning though reflection-in-context.

KLeOS (Knowledge and Learning Organisation System)

KLeOS (Vavoula, 2004) is a system designed to support the organization and management of learning across a lifetime. At the most basic level, KLeOS supports learning in performing activities, where each activity involves the usage or handling of one or more learning objects (physical or virtual). Activities are grouped together by thematic, temporal or spatial proximity to form learning episodes, and learning episodes are grouped into learning projects based on purposes and outcomes.

KLeOS presents the learner with a timeline of episodes that is linked to a concept map of their personal notes. The system provides a bridge between the timeline and the concept map by tagging knowledge nodes with the context of learning episodes. In this way, learners are supported in retrieving objects and knowledge based on both episodic and semantic learning memories. This type of reflection-on-context can assist learners in performing related activities and interpreting, using or reusing either the outcomes or process of their learning.

Interactive Logbook

The Interactive Logbook (Kiddie et al., 2004) is a personal learning environment designed to support university students engaged in both formal and informal learning activities. A host application on the desktop coordinates a range of plug-ins to access applications (e.g. a word processor) and services (e.g. email). A complementary mobile phone client provides access to a subset of these resources for learners on the move or with limited access to a desktop.

Like KLeOS, the Interactive Logbook provides a common interface to access a range of tools and resources that relate to a learner's learning. Through a combination of manual and automatic logging, all activities that take place in the logbook can be recorded and tagged with contextual information to create a portfolio of learning. Learners are supported in carrying out reflection-on-context through the provision of tools to filter, search, display and export parts of the portfolio to other applications. Log entries can also be linked to and organized by targets, providing support for forward planning. It is not the system that decides what contextual features are important; rather it is the learners who create their own context through their interactions with it.

The future of context awareness

Society is becoming increasingly mobile and connected, with a variety of information services and means of communication available to us wherever we go. We believe that mobility and context awareness are highly complementary. With the limited resources of mobile technology, as compared to desktop computers, and the limited attention of a learner on the move, it is even more important to design systems and services that are usable, useful and elegant. The widespread use of mobile technologies also opens up new possibilities for promoting collaborative construction of context, either explicitly (e.g. by student groups sharing notes during a lecture) or implicitly (e.g. by a system recognizing visitor paths, relating these to user profiles, and adapting the information it provides for future visitors).

Ultimately, all learning is personal and, in most cases, seamlessly integrated with daily life. Our goal is to design for a future where learning with technology is so integrated with daily life that it is not recognized as learning at all.

References

Bull, S. and A.T. McEvoy (2003), 'An Intelligent Learning Environment with an Open Learner Model for the Desktop PC and Pocket PC', in *International Journal of Artificial Intelligence in Education*, Amsterdam: IOS Press, pp. 389–391.

Kiddie, P., T. Marianczak, N. Sandle, L. Bridgefoot, C. Mistry, D, Williams, D. Corlett, M. Sharples and S. Bull (2004), *Interactive Logbook: The Development of an Application to Enhance and Facilitate Collaborative Working within Groups in Higher Education*, MLEARN 2004: Learning Anytime, Everywhere, Rome.

Lonsdale, P., C. Baber, M. Sharples and T.N. Arvanitis (2003), *A context-awareness architecture for facilitating mobile learning*, MLEARN 2003: Learning with Mobile Devices, London, LSDA.

Lonsdale, P., C. Baber, M. Sharples, W. Byrne, T.N. Arvanitis, P. Brundell and R. Beale (2004), *Context awareness for MOBIlearn: creating an engaging learning experience in an art museum*, MLEARN 2004: Learning Anytime, Everywhere, Rome.

Naismith, L., J. Ting and M. Sharples (2005), *CAERUS: A context aware educational resource system for outdoor sites*, CAL'05: Virtual Learning? University of Bristol, UK.

Sharples, M., N. Jeffery, J.B.H. du Boulay, D. Teather, B. Teather and G.H. du Boulay (2002), 'Socio-cognitive engineering: A methodology for the design of human-centred technology', in *European Journal of Operational Research* 136(2), pp. 310–323.

Vavoula, G.N. (2004), 'KLeOS: A Knowledge and Learning Organisation System in Support of Lifelong Learning', unpublished PhD Thesis, Electrical, Electronic and Computer Engineering, University of Birmingham, UK.

FOCUS GROUP DISCUSSION

20

Personalizing Learning: Is there a shared vision?

Sara de Freitas, Chris Dickinson and Chris Yapp

The following notes were the outcomes of the three break-out sessions held at the Design Council on 4 July 2005. The three groups focused upon the perceived impact of personalization upon policy, learners and teachers, and serve as a summary for the range of perspectives outlined in this volume.

Personalization and policy

Personalization means different things to different stakeholders, creating significant challenges for formulating a truly shared vision of what we mean by the term and what we want to achieve through this approach.

In general, however, there is some consensus that the term operates on a continuum: from customization to individualization to personalization, where personalizing learning is not simply about supporting the single learner, but rather about supporting collaborative learning through the use of services and interactive content from e-portfolios to integrated portal systems from educational games to sequenced learning objects. These innovative services have the potential to bring together learning content, advice and services to **support collaborative learning opportunities**.

Personalization in this context means more than choice and selection of what and where to learn; it means formalizing a commitment to bring different communities together to enrich and broaden the learner's experience, through **empowering the learner to take more control over what and how they learn**.

To achieve this broad objective, if it can be agreed upon, means supporting top-down strategic approaches, led by the Department of Education and Skills and other policy-making organizations, and bottom-up initiatives promoted by practitioners, researchers and learners in the field. This means careful **governance of strategic objectives** and creating 'buy in' from **these communities**, both of which involve supporting broadened objectives of our leaders, while creating simple messages to which the communities can all subscribe. Leadership is vital if learners are to be empowered sufficiently to achieve their learning objectives and quality is to be maintained through all levels of the learning journey.

In order to achieve this 'buy in' to a shared vision, **outcome benefits** need to be communicated to the community; **sustainability** needs to be guaranteed by a longer and more joined-up approach to development in the sector – this needs cross-party support; and **continuing professional development** needs to be provided and sustained over the longer term. In addition, spaces for collaboration need to be forged, and these spaces need to engage all the stakeholders, including: policy makers, research practitioners and experts, teaching practitioners, learners and business people, who need to be included in the dialogue that must occur in tandem with new developments.

Although we are still some distance from achieving a shared vision for personalization, and though we still need to establish the business case for supporting this approach, if we don't begin to forge this vision we face failing our learners, through developing flawed systems, widening the gap between the haves and have nots, and not providing industry with the calibre of workers that they need and expect. Therefore the need to develop this shared vision, create buy in from all the stakeholders and formulate an effective business case for this approach is critical to the success of our community, and for these reasons we need to continue to develop this work collaboratively, creating a simple message of **learner empowerment and equality** for all communities to work toward.

Personalization and the impact on learners

Inevitably the complexity of the concept of 'personalized learning' leads to the proliferation of questions, seemingly heretical.

The first question is *Why?* Are we looking at a solution to the deficiencies of online individualization or is it the latest government bandwagon? The impact on learners will differ accordingly. Indeed if the latter perception prevails, it is possible to conclude that the impact on learners will be insubstantial.

A second question is *Who?* Given resource constraints, certainly within the schools sector, it might become necessary to ask whether **personalized learning should be open to all** and if the answer is No, then to whom should it be available? Closely related to this is the question as to whether all learners want their learning personalized. Those adolescents, for instance, who go to great lengths to conform in their non-conformity, may, for social reasons, see personalized learning as a step too far. Clearly any rationing of provision will, by definition, result in differing levels of impact.

Thirdly comes the *What?* Simply stated does all learning have to be personalized and again if the answer is No, what distinguishes that which does from that which doesn't? One possible answer is that personalized learning is learning that meets a need and, therefore, **need defines the learning that has to be personalized**. The key question now becomes, Who defines the need? If the learner defines the need, a form of personalization occurs which permits of the possibility that realms of knowledge will not be accessed and rafts of competences will not be acquired. Given that 'getting on in life' is currently in a complex causal relationship with 'success in education' personalization properly implemented could impede development. Much depends here on the nature of assessment. Teachers teach to the test because test scores are how individual and institutional success is measured. To the extent that this happens in reality, it is the teacher who defines the need, and the learner therefore cannot, by definition, have their learning personalized. It is possible to conclude that the crux of the problem of personalizing learning in the compulsory education sector is that while personalizing is always done by the learner – that is, constructivism – teachers teaching to the test is inimical to constructivist approaches. From this it follows that the impact of personalizing learning on the learner will be dependent on some fundamental changes in the system, for example, testing, examinations, league tables, national strategies.

One possible conceptual way forward that may be helpful in teasing out the impact on learners is to distinguish three levels and two forms of personalization.

One form could be '**personalizing for**'. In practical terms this means customization. A teacher, lecturer or mentor of some kind, either virtual or real, will provide learning experiences that meet the need of a particular learner. The alternate form is '**personalizing by**'. In practical terms this means that the learner meets their own need by exercising choice.

The three levels of personalization define the areas within which choices are made and needs are to be met. In the 'personalizing for' form they can provide an agenda for negotiation between the learner and the provider. These three levels are: **goals**, **curriculum** and **environment**.

Viewed as a matrix, these two forms and three levels could be seen as providing a developmental continuum through which individuals progress. Thus, while children in the early years of their education may have a curriculum personalized for them, 18 year olds will be personalizing their own goals and adults will have taken charge of curriculum and environment in addition to goals.

In assuming a progression from 'personalizing for' to 'personalizing by' it will be necessary to identify those learner differences that impact on an individual's ability to succeed in their learning and provide the means by which learners can develop their learning style, habits, repertoire and literacies. Paradoxically, if learners are to benefit from personalized learning, they cannot negotiate out of learning how to learn.

Personalization and the impact on teachers

The rate at which the transformation of learning towards a more personalized system can be managed depends more on the rate at which the teaching profession can be remodelled and re-skilled than on any other factor. Today's teachers would argue, as many before them, that they aspire in their current practice to personalize learning for their students. They will argue that it is a lack of time and resources that is a constraint rather than a lack of will.

If this is to be tested as a proposition, then the key challenge is to free time for teachers to enable them to extend and explore their own skills to support enhanced personalization. How is this to be achieved?

The first step needs to be redefining the teacher as a learner, to focus on their own personalized needs as learners, and to use technologies as part of their own CPD so that they experience personalized learning and can reflect on this before being exposed in front of their students. Quite rightly, many teachers are concerned about 'experimenting' on a generation of pupils with what many will consider unproven or untested practices.

Everything that we might say about personalization for the learner will therefore equally apply to the teacher too.

In particular, **learning is a social and a socializing process**. Collaborative learning among teachers in a 'community of practice' should allow for the capture of both formal and informal knowledge and ideas to provide a richer dialogue within the profession to diffuse practice across the system. We would argue that there is no shortage of innovative practice within teaching today, but rather that it is the mechanism for diffusing that practice that is the major impediment.

This is the start of the journey, but it was felt that the support of individual learners would require, perhaps paradoxically, greater teamwork and collaboration among teachers. This would allow for new models of professionalism to emerge in time, supporting a wider range of roles than teacher, classroom assistant, Local Education Authority (LEA) advisor and so on.

Indeed, the remodelling of the profession allows us to challenge notions of what functions need to be performed within an individual institution, such as a college or school. Technology increasingly allows resources, digital and human, to be available to more than one institution.

This is why there is a central **need for the articulation and communication of a shared vision for new roles for teachers in the journey to personalization**. The clear danger is that with changes in curriculum, assessment and organizational governance, teachers may feel that they have less time, less power to manage their time to engage in transformation, so that professional inertia is or is perceived to be a blocker rather than an enabler of change.

Afterword

A Virtuous or Vicious Cycle of Learning Innovation: The digital choice facing education

A theme that has emerged from earlier discussions of e-learning (e.g. Nash *et al.*, 2004) is that the major barrier to progress in using ICTs for more effective learning is the absence of a clear and compelling vision – a mental model of the role of e-learning in the educational process. Contributors to this volume also identify this barrier, while offering a rich and informed picture of the key issues that arise from a vision of enabling students, teachers and others to choose and develop 'personalized learning' approaches using ICTs that can be tailored to the needs of specific individuals or groups. They also show how this vision is tied to the wider educational and social transformations that are emerging as people at all levels, and in all countries, make 'digital choices' about whether or not, and how, to use ICTs (Dutton, 2004).

A key digital choice facing educational institutions around the world relates to decisions about using ICTs like the Internet to replace other forms of learning, as in creating online sections of campus-based courses, or to complement classroom and other learning experiences by enabling students, teachers, administrators and parents to reconfigure their access to learning resources tailored to their particular needs.

It is important to recognize that certain choices reinforce e-learning trends, at all levels, which could further distance and depersonalize learning. For example, a number of major universities have created online lecture sessions for their campus-based students. Instead of a professor lecturing to hundreds in an auditorium, the professor would lecture to a smaller group of students in person, while hundreds of other campus-based students can only listen to Webcasts of the live session. Those students enrolled in the 'online' sections of the course can view the Webcast at the time and place they choose, but they cannot choose to sit in the live classroom. Rather than personalizing learning, this creates a further distancing of the learner by substituting mediated for real classroom experiences along with the motivational and other social benefits that these deliver. In being part of a potentially 'vicious cycle' of e-learning driven by a financial rather than educational paradigm, this threatens to realize the 'automated mass educational production line' nightmare of e-learning critics over the decades.

As de Freitas and Yapp (2005) suggest, countering such trends by using ICTs to complement and personalize existing learning resources will require active involvement in a long-term journey by many actors, from learners and teachers to institutional leaders and policy makers. They also point out: 'To sustain energy and momentum, to build successes and evidence to support the ongoing programme will require much greater feedback between all the "stakeholders".' The techno-economic imperatives to do otherwise are great but, as they note, the technology itself 'provides the capability to make this feedback easier, quicker and above all scalable'.

The Internet and other ICT-based networks can help to generate a 'virtuous cycle' of innovation encompassing such dynamic feedback. In this process, networks are one of the fruits of innovation and, in turn, a stimulus to further changes in the processes and tools of learning, for example in adopting more personalized modes of learning. Within this cycle, ICT-enabled networks play the crucial role of providing capabilities that not only make each learner feel they are at the centre of their own education and learning networks, but similarly place each teacher, parent, administrator, policy maker and other stakeholder at the heart of their own resources relevant to their roles in education and learning (Nash *et al.*, 2004).

Interactions within and between such networks could promote a dynamic, bottom-up model of adaptive change that encourages dialogue, reflection and adaptation between networks of players at all levels. This is vital, given the unpredictable, complex and rapid pace of education and learning change that is needed to keep pace with interrelated social, economic and technological changes.

As those at the centres of their interconnected networks adapt learning processes and practices to meet different pedagogic, economic, administrative, political, ethical and other real-world requirements, transformations can occur over time by complementing, and at times replacing, some learning and related institutional practices and policies. This network model of communication also offers an alternative to the unhelpful dichotomy that has led to the seemingly eternal battle between the two main competing learning paradigms: a 'traditional' one-to-many, teacher-centred classroom instruction versus student-centred, activity-based learning in which the teacher acts more as a facilitator than instructor.

The network model suggested by the concept of personalization brings to teachers, students and other learners a new array of possibilities from which to select, in order to reconfigure their access to: people (students, teachers, parents, and so on); information (sources of content); services (e-learning software, simulation, expert advice, and so on); and ICTs (in classrooms, homes, libraries, and so on). It can accommodate either of the other main models, where that is appropriate for local actors. At the same time, it creates new pathways for e-learning innovations, such as new forms of peer reviewing, sharing teaching and learning experiences or gaining information and advice from peers, experts and other sources, on a local or global scale.

Such networks can be informal as well as formal and encompass real and virtual communities involving many actors in a variety of new forms of interaction, such as: within and between teachers and learners; among parents and between parents and schools; or between universities and local communities and businesses. Ultralab projects such as NotSchool (see Moss, 2005) illustrate the kinds of innovative pathways this opens for exploration.

A network model has important policy implications. For instance, it offers a means of bottom-up learning innovation without the top-down imposition of a particular educational approach. If this is deemed to be appropriate, it could be supported by shifting the focus of public policy from creating e-learning content to a greater emphasis on providing social, personal, technical and financial incentives and backing for a diverse range of networking initiatives that will be taken forward largely by the people involved in the networks. Bottom-up adaptive change is also more likely to have a realistic chance of successful widespread implementation because change initiatives are more likely to go with the motivational grain of different actors and groups as they negotiate outcomes.

Achieving the full benefits of ICT-enabled network interactions within and across such local and global communities will obviously depend increasingly on providing the greater equity of network access necessary to extend the reach of high-quality educational resources across social, geographic and economic divides. This is essential for realizing an ultimate goal of learning personalization: to make appropriate learning experiences available wherever the learner happens to be, at the time of their choosing, in ways they find most appealing – and with the support of teachers, institutions, parents and all others who care about the outcomes.

William H. Dutton
Director, Oxford Internet Institute

References

de Freitas, S. and Yapp, C. (2005), 'Introduction to the Contributions – Personalization: Is there a consensus?', in S. de Freitas and C. Yapp (eds) *Personalizing Learning in the 21st Century*, Stafford: Network Educational Press, pp. xi–xiii.

Dutton, W.H. (2004), *Social Transformation in the Information Society*. Paris: UNESCO Publications for the WSIS.

Moss, M. (2005), 'Personalized Learning: A failure to collaborate?', in S. de Freitas and C. Yapp (eds) *Personalizing Learning in the 21st Century*, Stafford: Network Educational Press, pp. 67–71.

Nash, V., W.H. Dutton and M. Peltu (2004), 'Innovative Pathways to the Next Level of e-Learning: OII Forum Discussion Paper No. 2', Oxford: Oxford Internet Institute. See http://www.oii.ox.ac.uk/resources/publications/FD2.pdf.

About the Authors

Editors

Sara de Freitas

Dr Sara de Freitas currently works as a Research Fellow in ICT and Education based at the London Knowledge Lab – a collaborative venture between Birkbeck College and the Institute of Education, University of London. Sara also consults with the UK Joint Information Systems Committee e-Learning Development Programme in the Innovation strand, exploring the applications and developments of innovative technologies upon post-16 learning. Sara also founded and co-chairs the UK Lab Group, which brings the research and development community together to create stronger links between industrial and academic research and development. Her current post involves project managing the development of a personalized portal system for supporting the career and educational choices of lifelong learners in London.

As well as publishing widely in the areas of pedagogy and e-learning, change management and strategy development for implementing e-learning systems, and educational games and electronic simulations for supporting post-16 training and learning, Sara is also on the editorial board of an international journal, sits on international conference boards and supports ICT and educational initiatives in the developing world. Sara has also worked on a range of expert consultations including a Department of Trade and Industry Collaborative Research and Development award for developing serious gaming applications for training.

Chris Yapp

Dr Chris Yapp is Head of Public Sector Innovation at Microsoft. Chris has worked in the IT industry for 25 years in a variety of roles. His long-term interests have been in Networking and Education and he has specialized in the areas of lifelong learning, e-government, the creative industries and social exclusion in the emerging knowledge society. He is a frequent public speaker on strategic issues around IT and has been a member of a number of Government Advisory Groups. He is an Associate of the Think Tank DEMOS, a Trustee of the educational charity MirandaNet and a Patron of the National Association for Able Children in Education, NACE.

Contributors

Keynote contributor

Diana Laurillard

Professor Diana Laurillard is Head of the e-Learning Strategy Unit at the UK Government's Department for Education and Skills and is Visiting Professor at The Open University and the Institute of Education. She is responsible for developing a coherent e-strategy for the DfES across all the education and skills sectors, including schools, post-16, higher education, adult learning, training, home-based learning, workplace learning and partnerships with private suppliers. The strategy, *Harnessing Technology: Transforming Learning and Children's Services*, was published in March 2005.

Professor Laurillard previously held two terms of office as Pro-Vice-Chancellor at the Open University. During that period she was responsible for developing the appropriate use of learning technologies within the full range of learning and teaching methods in the University's courses, and for the structural reform at the heart of its course production operations. By the end of her second term, over 160,000 students were connecting online to the OU for aspects of their study, and over half the courses had integrated e-learning with more traditional methods. Her academic work spans more than 25 years of research, development and evaluation of interactive multimedia materials and internet services in education and training, covering a wide range of discipline areas. Her book *Rethinking University Teaching* (Routledge Falmer, 2nd edn., 2002), has been widely acclaimed and is still used as a set book for courses on learning technology all over the world. She has been a member of the Visiting Committee on IT at Harvard University and a member of the Dearing Committee on Higher Education for the UK Government. This work has been recognized through her honorary degrees from the University of Abertay and the Open University of the Netherlands. She is a Fellow of the Royal Society of Arts and an Honorary Fellow of University College London.

From 1 September 2005 Diana will take up a new Chair in Learning with Digital Technologies at the London Knowledge Lab, launched in 2004 jointly by the Institute of Education and Birkbeck College.

Other contributors

Rob Arntsen

Rob Arntsen has extensive experience in the learning technology industry and in general management. He was part of IBM for 22 years, before leaving in March 2000 to form MyKnowledgeMap. He held a number of senior management positions within IBM, including Learning Technologies Solutions Manager for Europe, Middle East and Africa, Northern Region Manager for General Business Division, and UK Manager of New Markets.

He was appointed as a member of the National Advisory Council for Continuous Education and Lifelong Learning, Technology Working Group and served as a member of the Working Group on Widening Participation by the Council for Industry and Higher Education. He was a member of the original IPPR group that produced the proposal for the University for Industry. He was also a member of the CBI Regional Council for Yorkshire and Humberside for many years.

Most recently, in 2005, Rob was part of the LSDA national steering group on Innovation in Teaching and Learning. He is also a governor and Chair of Audit of a large FE college.

Graeme Atherton

Dr Graeme Atherton has been Manager of the Aimhigher Central London Partnership since January 2005. Prior to this role, he was the Associate Dean of Widening Participation at Liverpool Hope University College and was closely involved with Aimhigher in Greater Merseyside. Aimhigher's work relates closely to his past and previous research interests. His doctorate study examined the experiences of adults with few or no qualifications returning to education in Liverpool. His recent research has focused on the impact of widening participation initiatives on the attitudes of young people from backgrounds under-represented in HE and the political context of the drive to increase the numbers of young people in HE. In recent years he has delivered papers on these themes to international conferences in several European countries and in the United States.

Bob Banks

Dr Bob Banks has worked for many years with ICT in education, as a teacher, researcher, developer, and consultant. He is currently a senior consultant with Tribal Technology, where he has played a leading role in the development of learndirect's managed learning environment and Tribal's e-learning product set.

He was a lead researcher in the 'RENAISSANCE', 'GESTALT' and 'GAIA' European collaborative research projects and has written a number of papers on pedagogic and organizational aspects of e-learning. Arising from this, he has contributed to a number of global e-learning standards initiatives. He was awarded a PhD for research on neural networks and has worked on related areas such as computer-supported collaborative working and digital library systems.

Bob is passionately committed to the potential of new technology to empower learners and to support new kinds of learning communities.

Helen Beetham

Helen Beetham is Research Consultant to the Joint Information Systems Committee's e-Learning Programme, developing and supporting the JISC's activities in e-Learning and pedagogy. Previously a Research Fellow in e-learning at the Open University, she is widely published and a regular speaker at conferences in the UK and abroad.

Her research and publication interests include: learning design, organizational change, e-learning and educational theory (particularly activity theory), models of effective practice and effective learning, e-portfolios and personal development.

She has contributed to a wide range of nationally-funded research and development projects in e-learning, for bodies including the JISC, SHEFC, HEFCE, the DfES, the HE Academy and Subject Centres, Becta, the Centre for Recording Achievement, the Association of Learning Technologies and the Oxford Centre for Staff and Learning Development. Helen has been involved in staff and educational development for e-learning since 1997. She was a Senior Lecturer in Educational Development at the University of Plymouth and has contributed to e-learning strategies at several other HEIs. She regularly advises departments on the development of effective, subject-based and pedagogically sound approaches to e-learning.

Tim Bilham

Tim Bilham is Director of Education Research and Development in the School for Health at the University of Bath.

He leads the team responsible for the design, development and evaluation of postgraduate programmes for health, medical and social care professionals delivered using innovative approaches to blended and e-learning. These include inter-professional programmes at doctoral and Masters level and courses that widen access for disadvantaged learners. He established, and is Director of Studies for, the University's first online MSc in Healthcare Informatics, developed in partnership with the Royal College of Surgeons of Edinburgh. He recently won an Innovations in Learning and Teaching Award for his work in delivering online education for medical practitioners.

A Cambridge graduate in mathematics and engineering science, with considerable experience in lifelong learning, Tim has acted as a consultant to a number of international organizations and was project director for two major international development projects establishing new Colleges of Open and Distance Education in Botswana and Namibia. His interests are in the development of organizational capability for distance education, the design of online learning and methodologies for the development of effective online communities of practice.

Tim Brighouse

Professor Tim Brighouse is presently Chief Adviser for London Schools and visiting professor at the Institute of Education at London University.

Until September 2002 he was Chief Education Officer in Birmingham for nearly ten years. Earlier he was Professor of Education at Keele University (1989–93), Chief Education Officer of Oxfordshire (1978–89) and Deputy Education Officer in the ILEA. He was brought up in East Anglia, attended state schools and read history at Oxford University before embarking on a career in education and teaching in grammar and secondary modern schools. He entered the world of educational administration in what was Monmouthshire and served in Buckinghamshire and with the Association of County Councils.

Tim has written extensively, especially on school improvement, and has a number of books and articles to his name. He has also broadcast on radio and television and has spoken at many national and international conferences. He has also contributed articles to the Political Quarterly and the Oxford Review of Education. Tim is author of *What makes a Good School* and *How to Improve Your School*.

Tim has received honorary doctorates from The Open University, University of Central England, Oxford Brookes University, Exeter University, Warwick University, Birmingham University, University of the West of England and Sheffield Hallam University.

He is married and has four children who are now grown up. He supports Oxford United.

Sarah Davies

Sarah Davies has worked in educational technology for many years and is currently Programme Manager for the Distributed e-learning programme at JISC. Previously she managed the National Grid for Learning portal at Becta, worked as a learning technologist in higher education and managed the development of educational software for schools. As with most people, entering this field was an accident, caused by a deviation from linguistics to the use of speech technology in language learning. However, it's been a pretty interesting accident.

Chris Dickinson

Chris Dickinson trained as a teacher of history and geography and has spent 20 years working in education in Cambridge, West Yorkshire and Somerset. His last school-based job was as a member of the Senior Management Team at Priory School, Weston-super-Mare, where he had responsibility for continuing professional development. At this time the school became involved in the Department of Employment's Flexible Learning Project and Chris's role in this led on to work with the County of Avon's TVEI Project, eventually becoming Regional Co-ordinator for this in the South West. When this project came to an end, Chris co-founded Network Educational Press Ltd and has been Chairman of the company since 1991.

Chris is the author of two books and numerous articles. *Differentiation: a handbook of classroom strategies* was published by NCET and *Effective Learning Activities* was published by Network Educational Press Ltd. He is well regarded as a conference speaker and INSET presenter and is noted for his ability to convey complex ideas in a down-to-earth, humorous way.

William Dutton

William H. Dutton (BA, University of Missouri, M.A., PhD, SUNY Buffalo) is Director of the Oxford Internet Institute and Professor of Internet Studies at the University of Oxford, where he is also a Fellow of Balliol College. Until joining Oxford in July 2002, he was a Professor in the Annenberg School for Communication at the University of Southern California. At USC, he was elected President of the Faculty, presiding over USC's Academic Senate during 2000–01. In the UK, prior to directing the OII, William was a Fulbright Scholar (1986–87), and later the

National Director of the UK's successful Programme on Information and Communication Technologies (PICT) from 1993 to 1996. Among his recent publications on the social aspects of information and communication technologies are *Society on the Line* (Oxford University Press, 1999), *Digital Academe: New Media in Higher Education and Learning*, edited with Brian D. Loader (Taylor & Francis Routledge, 2002), *Transforming Enterprise*, edited with Brian Kahin and others (MIT Press, 2004) and a monograph for the World Summit on the Information Society, entitled *Social Transformation in an Information Society* (Paris: UNESCO, 2004).

Tom Franklin

Tom Franklin has worked in learning technology for over ten years and has been particularly concerned with user needs in the design and implementation of systems. This has led to work on virtual and managed learning environments and portals. He currently believes that VLEs only have a limited shelf-life and will be replaced by portals that offer better functionality for users and better integration. He has also worked in accessibility and usability – he was responsible for the formation of TechDis – and in standards, where he was responsible for the creation of CETIS. He is now an independent consultant providing strategic advice on the use of portals and the integration of systems, as well as VLEs and MLEs.

Tom Holland

Dr Tom Holland has worked for MyKnowledgeMap since October 2004. He previously attended the University of York, where he wrote his PhD on the influence of crowd psychology on modernist aesthetics. He has published articles on literacy and self-education in the early twentieth century and has several years' teaching experience in higher education.

Since he arrived at MyKnowledgeMap, Tom has played a leading role in editing and creating learning content and was involved in the development of the Retail Detail service for the Retail Academy.

Niel McLean

After 15 years in teaching, LEA advisory work and consultancy work for a number of curriculum and assessment projects, Niel McLean joined the School Curriculum and Assessment Authority for the 'Dearing review' of the National Curriculum in England. He led on assessment work in IT and D&T, being responsible for all areas of examinations and qualifications in those areas, continuing to be responsible for ICT at QCA.

He joined Becta in 1998 as Director for Schools where he led on its curriculum, LEA support and inclusion work. He established Becta's Evidence and Practice directorate. Niel has led on establishing Becta as a focus for educational research on ICT and good practice, including developing Becta's successful awards schemes, managing significant research projects such as Impact 2 and establishing Becta's ICT Research Network. Becta is regularly called on to provide advice on ICT in education to both policy makers and practitioners. Under Niel's lead, Becta has established itself as a focus for online communities of practitioners sharing and developing approaches to teaching and learning.

Niel has recently become Executive Director, Educational Practice and now has overall responsibility for Institutional Development and Teaching and Learning at Becta.

Alistair McNaught

Alistair McNaught has 19 years teaching experience in FE and five years in 11–18 education. A geography teacher by trade, he has been involved in using e-learning in mainstream teaching since the mid-1990s. He worked part time as ILT co-ordinator at Peter Symonds' College for three years, contributing to a wide range of subject-based projects and a project with the Science Museum. He has worked as a freelance author and has been involved in staff development for nearly a decade. He was involved with Becta's FERL team in the writing and delivery of both the ILT Champions Programme and the Ferl Practitioner's Programme. He also worked with a range of Regional Support Centres on developing subject-based interactive materials across a wide range of subjects and levels. In 2004 he joined TechDis as Senior Advisor for FE.

Rachada Monthienvichienchai

Rachada Monthienvichienchai's current area of interest is the pedagogy of personalized online learning. His main research focuses on designing e-learning solutions for individual differences in the learner's characteristics and fostering of communities of practice through online learning environments and activities. Rachada's earlier work was concerned with the use of rich-media learning content to support vicarious learning in higher education. His present position is the Institute of Education's (University of London) Principal Research Officer for the iClass project – an EU-funded Framework 6 Integrated Project. He holds a PhD in Computer Science from University College London and has lectured there since 2000. He has also acted as Educational Technology consultant for St John's University and St John's International School, Bangkok, since 1998.

Malcolm Moss

Before his current role as Principal Facilitator at Ultralab, Malcolm Moss was a teacher of 11–18 year olds involved with design technology, computers in education, enterprise and business links. He ran or contributed to teacher training courses as an Essex LEA associate tutor and in 1997 established an international internet project which continues to engage teachers and students.

After a series of secondments to local sixth forms and sponsorships by national agencies there was an extended secondment to HTI (Heads and Teachers into Industry) as an adviser for Tesco SchoolNet 2000, after which he joined Ultralab. Initially he worked on the Talking Heads project, an online community for headteachers, on behalf of the DfES and now an established part of the National College for School Leadership's online provision. His contribution centred on headteacher links with DfES ministers and officials and on establishing localized online networks of headteachers.

He has been involved in many Ultralab projects since then, mainly associated with online education and – particularly – assessment. These include Ultraversity (an online BA Hons degree in learning technology and research), ICDC, eViva and COGS. All feature assessment for learning and Ultralab's philosophy of delightful learning.

Currently he is working in partnership with other national agencies on a fully e-assessed 16+ examination. This project also incorporates teacher professional development to support the fundamental changes required in teaching and learning.

Laura Naismith

Laura Naismith is a Research Associate at the University of Birmingham's Centre for Educational Technology and Distance Learning (CETADL). She has been funded by Microsoft for three years to research products and solutions in the areas of educational technology and distance learning. Her current research interests include the design of mobile technology to support learning in museums and the design of technology to support continuing professional development. Her recent publications include an activity-based literature review of mobile technologies and learning, commissioned by NESTA Futurelab.

John Sewell

John Sewell is an engineer who got into accessibility as a volunteer making aids for students at the National Star College. Later he dovetailed a career in local and national politics with working part time for the college, making and adapting equipment for individuals. When the political career came to an end he became full time at the college, taking up teaching IT as well. Eventually he became the manager of the college's Karten Open Learning Centre and took on responsibility for e-learning and access. He was nominated to sit on the Specialist College ILT group of the LSC, which looked at how the sector could improve its provision and use of IT and e-learning. In 2004 he joined TechDis as Senior Advisor for Specialist Colleges.

Ros Smith

Ros Smith has been an Education Officer at Becta and a member of the Ferl team, with responsibility for e-learning, quality and inspection in the post-16 sector before leaving to work full time as a consultant and writer on e-learning for the e-Learning and Pedagogy strand of the JISC e-Learning Programme. Project manager and co-author for *Effective Practice with e-Learning* (JISC, 2004), Ros has now overseen the production of its partner publication *Innovative Practice with e-Learning* from the e-Learning and Innovation strand.

Ros has also written the Becta guide to inspection and e-learning, *Demonstrating Transformation* (Becta, 2004), and acted as adviser to the Education and Training Inspectorate of Northern Ireland (eti) in the production of guidelines to colleges on the effective use of e-learning technologies in the Improving Quality, Raising Standards Framework for the inspection of further education programmes in Northern Ireland. During 2003–04, Ros chaired the Becta Raising Standards Steering Group and actively promoted the understanding of effective practice in e-learning among all UK inspectorates.

Shane Sutherland

Shane Sutherland is the e-Portfolio Project Director at the University of Wolverhampton and Director of Pebble Learning, the spin-out company responsible for the development of the PebblePAD e-Portfolio system.

Shane previously worked at Wolverhampton's School of Education, before moving to the Centre for Learning and Teaching as an e-Mentor. He is particularly enthusiastic about taming technology to make its power accessible to teachers and students to support the process of learning.

Despite his busy schedule, Shane still finds time to teach in areas as diverse as the PGCert HE, first-year undergraduate studies and sailing! Throughout the year Shane also runs e-Learning Retreats for fellow teachers, exploring the innovative use of e-Portfolios, Virtual Learning Environments, WebQuests and other web-based systems.

John West-Burnham

Professor John West-Burnham works as a teacher, writer and consultant in leadership development. He is Senior Research Adviser at the National College for School Leadership.

He worked in schools and further and adult education for 15 years before moving into higher education and was also a part-time Open University tutor for 15 years. He has worked at Crewe and Alsager College, the University of Leicester, the University of Lincolnshire and Humberside, the University of Hull and the London Leadership Centre. He was also Development Officer for Teacher Performance for Cheshire LEA. John is author of *Managing Quality in Schools*; co-author of *Effective Learning in Schools*, *Leadership and Professional Development in Schools* and *Personalizing Learning: Transforming Education*; and co-editor of *Performance Management in Schools*, *Educational Leadership and the Community*, *The Handbook of Educational Leadership and Management*. He has also written 12 other books and over 30 articles and chapters.

John has worked in Australia, Cyprus, the Czech Republic, Estonia, Germany, Holland, Israel, New Zealand, Norway, the Republic of Ireland, Singapore, South Africa, Thailand, UAE and the USA. He is coordinator of the European School Leadership Project.

John's current research and writing interests include transformational leadership, leadership learning and development, and educational leadership in the community. He is Senior Visiting Research Fellow, Faculty of Education, University of Manchester; Visiting Professor at Liverpool Hope University and the University of Cyprus; and Visiting Professorial Associate at the Regional Training Unit, Northern Ireland.

Derek Wise

Derek Wise has been Head of Cramlington Community High School for 14 years. In 1999–2000 he was seconded for a year to Newcastle EAZ as Project Director. He is the co-author of two books: *Creating an Accelerated learning School* (2001), which uses the school as a case study for the introduction of accelerated learning, and *Accelerated Learning: A User's Guide* (2003).

Cramlington High School is a 13–18 High School of some 1600 students, with a fully comprehensive intake. It is a Specialist Science School. It was described by OFSTED in 2001 as 'A strikingly successful school' and 'an exciting place to learn'. It was highlighted as an outstanding school by (Her Majesty's Chief Inspector) HMCI and in 2003 was designated Leading Edge status. Its value added at Key Stage 4 puts it into the top 5 per cent of schools nationwide.

Index

Lightning Source UK Ltd.
Milton Keynes UK
UKOW07f0833130815

256863UK00002B/37/P

9 781855 392021